Wiggle & Wonder

Bible Story Rhymes AND Finger Plays

ILLUSTRATIONS BY
DANA REGAN

CONCORDIA PUBLISHING HOUSE · SAINT LOUIS

Illustrations by Dana Regan

Written by Jeanette Dall, Lorraine Groth, Corrie Klatt, Gail Pawlitz, Diane Tinker, and Marilyn Wiesehan

Some finger plays originally published in Our Life in Christ® © CPH and Growing in Christ® © CPH.

Edited by Lorraine Groth

All Scripture quotations are from the ESV Bible® (The Holy Bible, English Standard Version®), copyright © 2001 by Crossway Bibles, a publishing ministry of Good News Publishers. Used by permission. All rights reserved.

Manufactured in the United States of America

1 2 3 4 5 6 7 8 9 10   21 20 19 18 17 16 15 14 13 12

Contents

Introduction

Purpose	6
Tips for Success	6

PART 1: SUNDAY SCHOOL TIME

Transitions and Wiggles Out

Jump for Joy	7
Clap for Jesus	8
Wiggles Out	8
Jesus Is with Us	8
My Body	9
Clean Up	9
Time to Listen	10
Focusing Attention	10

Learning about God

I'm Glad	11
Learning about Jesus	11
Jesus Knows My Name	12
Church Manners	12
God's House	13
I'm Sorry	13

Prayers

Jesus Listens	14
When I Pray	14
Thank-You Litany	15
Thank You, God	15
Loving Hands	15

Church Year

Church-Year Colors	16
Advent	17
Advent Counting	17
Advent Waiting	17
Christmas	18
Epiphany	18
Lent	19
Palm Sunday	19
Good Friday	19
Easter Day	20
Ascension	20
Pentecost	21
Holy Trinity	21
St. Michael and All Angels	22
Reformation Day	22
All Saints' Day	23

Apostles' Creed

God the Father	23
Jesus, God's Son	24
God the Holy Spirit	25

God's Care

God Is Good to Me	26
God Is with Me	26
God Cares for Me	27
God Gives Me	27
Jesus Loves Me	27

Bible Words

God's Word	28
Here Is the Bible	28

Snack Time

Thank You, God	29
Thank You for Our Food	29
Thanks	29

Going Home

Good-bye	30
Closing Prayer	30

The Story of Creation

God Creates the World 31
God Creates Adam and Eve 32

The Fall and the Flood

Sin Enters the World 33
Cain and Abel 34
Noah and the Flood 35
Rainbow Hug 36
Noah, Noah, What Do You See? 36

Abraham and Isaac

God Calls Abraham 37
Abraham Rescues Lot 37
God's Covenant with Abraham 38
Abraham's Visitors from Heaven 38
Abraham Believes 39
The Birth of Isaac 39
Abraham and Isaac 40
Isaac and Rebekah 41

Jacob's Story

Jacob and Esau 42
Jacob's Dream 43
Jacob's Family 44
God Gives Families 45
Esau Forgives Jacob 45

Joseph and His Family

Joseph and His Brothers 46
Joseph's Troubles 47
Joseph Helps Pharaoh 48
Joseph Forgives 49

Moses and the Exodus

The Birth of Moses 50
Moses and the Burning Bush 51
Moses and the Plagues 52
The Passover 54
Crossing the Red Sea 55

Israel in the Wilderness

God Provides Manna and Quail 56
The Ten Commandments 57

Worship in the Tabernacle 58
The Twelve Spies in Canaan 58
The Bronze Serpent 59

Israel in the Promised Land

Crossing the Jordan 60
The Fall of Jericho 61
Deborah 62
Gideon 63
Samson 64
Ruth 65
God's Servant Samuel 65
Saul Becomes King 66

God Chooses David

David and Goliath 67
David and Jonathan 68
David Becomes King 69
Nathan and David 70

Great Prophets and Kings

Solomon Builds the Temple 71
Jonah 72
King Hezekiah Prays 73

Elijah and Elisha

God Cares for Elijah 74
Elijah and the Prophets of Baal 75
God Takes Elijah to Heaven 76
Hoorah for E! 76
Naaman and Elisha 77
Naaman Refrain 77

God's People in Exile

Three Men in the Fiery Furnace 78
Daniel in the Lions' Den 78
Esther 79

The Christmas Story

Birth of John Foretold 80
The Annunciation 80
Mary Visits Elizabeth 81
The Birth of John 82
An Angel Visits Joseph 82
The Birth of Jesus 83

Christmas Night 84
Baby Jesus 84
Here Is the Stable 84
The Presentation of Jesus 85
The Visit of the Wise Men 86
Young Jesus 86
The Boy Jesus in the Temple 87

Jesus and John the Baptist

John Prepares the Way 88
The Baptism of Jesus 88
The Temptation of Jesus 89

Jesus and the Disciples

Jesus Calls the First Disciples 90
Jesus Calls Philip and Nathanael 91
Jesus Calls Matthew 92
Matthew 92
Jesus Changes Water into Wine 93
Jesus Teaches Nicodemus 94
Jesus and the Samaritan Woman 95

Jesus Does Many Miracles

Jesus Rejected at Nazareth 96
Jesus Heals Many 97
Jesus Heals a Paralyzed Man 98
Jesus Calms a Storm 99
Jesus Heals Jairus's Daughter 100
Jesus Walks on Water 101
The Transfiguration 102
Jesus Heals a Blind Man 103

Jesus Teaches and Preaches

The Beatitudes 104
Jesus Clears the Temple 105
Jesus Tells about God's Care 106
Jesus Feeds Five Thousand 106
Jesus Is Anointed 107
Jesus Sends Out Seventy-two 108
The Good Samaritan 109
Jesus, the Good Shepherd 110
Jesus Teaches Us to Pray 111
Jesus Raises Lazarus 112

Jesus Goes to the Cross

The Prodigal Son 113
Jesus Heals Ten Men with Leprosy 114
Jesus Heals Ten Sick Men 115

Jesus and the Little Children 116
Jesus and Zacchaeus 117
The Widow's Mite 118
Jesus Gives the Lord's Supper 119
Peter Denies Jesus 120
Jesus Dies and Lives Again 121

Jesus Rises from the Grave

Easter Morning 122
The Empty Tomb 123
Jesus Appears to Mary Magdalene 124
Jesus Appears on the Emmaus Road 125
Jesus Appears to Thomas 126
Jesus Reinstates Peter 127
Jesus Ascends into Heaven 128

The Holy Spirit Leads the Apostles

God Sends the Holy Spirit 129
Peter and John Heal the Lame Man 130
God's Servant Stephen 131
Philip and the Ethiopian 132
Dorcas 133
Peter and Cornelius 134
Peter's Escape from Prison 135

Paul's Mission and Letters

The Conversion of Paul 136
Paul and Barnabas 137
Paul and Timothy 137
Lydia Is Baptized 138
Paul and Silas in Prison 139
Philemon 140
Paul Sails for Rome 141
The Bible Tells Us So 142

Heaven Is Our Home

John's Vision of Heaven 143

INTRODUCTION

Purpose

Wiggle & Wonder is chock-full of educationally appropriate activities that will reinforce scriptural truths for young children in an engaging and enjoyable way. Because finger plays involve repetition, movement, patterning, cadence, and focusing attention—all key ways that young children process information—these activities will also help children better learn and remember the Bible stories.

Part 1 has finger plays and litanies for Sunday School time that you will use over and over! These include rhymes and movement activities for openings and closings, prayers, snack time, transitions, and the Church Year, as well as ones that teach about our triune God and His love and care for us in Jesus.

Part 2 has finger plays and other active ways to teach and reinforce learning for many familiar Bible stories. While the book is designed primarily for use in a Sunday School setting, teachers in early childhood programs and Christian day schools, as well as parents at home, will find it an invaluable resource. To extend learning in these settings, there are suggested activities on each page linking the rhymes with skills that are taught throughout an early childhood curriculum.

Tips for Success

Kids like finger plays, rhymes, and other activities, especially when they can join in the fun. Here are a few things you'll want to remember to keep them interested and involved:

- Keep the children's abilities in mind and set realistic expectations. Some of the finger plays may work better with older children or may need to be shortened to just a few key lines for young children.

- Practice the finger play ahead of time until the words and actions feel comfortable and familiar. Feel free to change any words that are difficult and simplify the suggested actions.

- Speak slowly and with expression to help children focus on what you are saying. Emphasize the action words, and use exaggerated actions that the children can see. Encourage the children to imitate what you are doing.

- Do not be concerned if children don't join in right away, however, and never force participation.

- First, say the finger play with actions, allowing the children to observe. Then, repeat the finger play, teaching it in manageable sections. Repeat the actions with the children a few times so they become comfortable in doing them too. Teach them repetitive refrains and have them say those with you.

- Use the Bible story finger plays to review the Bible story. Speak and act reverently. The children will imitate your attitude and actions.

TRANSITIONS AND WIGGLES OUT

Jump for Joy

Jump, jump, jump for joy!
Jump.

Jesus loves each girl and boy.
Point to others.

Jump, jump, jump so high;
Jump.

Jesus came from heaven to die.
Point up.

Jump, jump, jump all day;
Jump.

So once more we all shall say:
Cup hands around mouth.

Jump, jump, jump for joy!
Jump.

Jesus loves each girl and boy.
Point to others.

VOCABULARY DEVELOPMENT
Substitute other action words for "jump," such as clap, skip, and wave. Do the appropriate action.

Clap for Jesus

Clap hands each time you say, "Clap, clap, clap."

Clap your hands if Jesus loves you.
   Clap, clap, clap.
Clap your hands if you're forgiven.
   Clap, clap, clap.
Clap your hands if Jesus loves you.
   Clap, clap, clap.
Clap your hands if you're going to
   heaven. Clap, clap, clap.

BODY AWARENESS
Substitute other actions, such as "Touch your knees," "Jump on one foot," or "Pat your head." Do the corresponding action.

Wiggles Out

Clap your hands—clap, clap, clap.
   Clap.

Jump in the air—jump, jump, jump.
   Jump.

Stomp your feet—stomp, stomp, stomp.
   Stomp.

Turn around once—turn, turn, turn.
   Turn around.

Walk to your seat—walk, walk, walk.
   Walk in place.

Sit down quietly—shh, shh, shh.
   Touch index finger to lips.

MOVEMENT
Do the actions named in the poem. Have the children suggest others.

Jesus Is with Us

Clap your hands for Jesus, 1, 2, 3.
   He loves you, and He loves me.
   Clap.

Stomp your feet for Jesus; He's our King.
   He protects from evil things!
   Stomp.

Wave your arms for Jesus, left and right.
   He is with us day and night!
   Wave arms.

MUSIC
Give children rhythm instruments to play. Change the words; for example, "Blow your horn for Jesus, 1, 2, 3," "Beat your drum for Jesus; He's our King," or "Shake your cymbals for Jesus, left and right."

My Body

I have a very special gift;
> *Point to self.*

Look what it can do!
> *Point to eyes.*

It helps me jump up, oh, so high.
> *Jump.*

It helps me bend down low.
> *Bend.*

It helps me walk. It helps me run.
> *Walk in place.*

It even helps me see.
> *Point to eyes.*

It's my body—head to toes!
> *Touch toes.*

God gave me ME!
> *Point to self.*

BODY AWARENESS
Have children identify different body parts and what each part does.

Clean Up

Clean, clean, clean the room.
> Put your things away.
>> *Pretend to pick up toys.*

Help, help, help, help—
> Then we'll sing and pray.
>> *Beckon with arm; fold hands in prayer.*

BEHAVIOR MODIFICATION
Use this rhyme to teach children to work together to achieve a goal. Use it at the end of free time before the lesson begins. It can be sung to the tune of "Row, Row, Row Your Boat."

Time to Listen

Here comes the kangaroo hopping along.
Hop.

Here comes the elephant, big and strong.
Sway bent arm like elephant trunk.

God made all the animals, big and small.
Hold hands wide apart and then close together.

He watches over them, one and all.
Shade eyes with hand; look around.

Stand up tall like a big oak tree.
Hold arms out like tree branches.

Buzz around like a bumblebee.
Flap arms.

Wiggle your elbows; wiggle your nose.
Wiggle nose with finger.

Bend down low, and touch your toes.
Touch toes.

Sit back down. Don't say a word.
Touch index finger to lips.

It's time to listen to God's Word.
Point to ears.

SOUND RECOGNITION
Have children take turns making animal sounds for the others
to guess.

Focusing Attention

Wiggle your fingers way up high.
Wiggle fingers above head.

Wiggle your fingers way down low.
Wiggle fingers down by knees.

Wiggle your fingers into your lap.
Wiggle fingers on lap.

Then fold them quietly—just so.
Fold hands.

LISTENING
Do this rhyme to prepare the children to listen to the Bible
words or story.

~~~~~~~~~~~~~~~~~~~

**LEARNING
ABOUT GOD**

~~~~~~~~~~~~~~~~~~~

I'm Glad

I'm glad to be in Sunday School.
Smile and hug self.

That's where my friends will be.
Point to children.

I'm glad to see my teacher,
Smile and hug self.

Who smiles when she sees me.
Point to corners of mouth as you smile.

I'm glad to be in Sunday School.
Smile and hug self.

It's a very happy place.
Twirl or spin, arms out.

I'm glad to learn about Jesus.
Smile and hug self.

His love puts a smile on my face.
Point to corners of mouth as you smile.

CRITICAL THINKING
Have children name two favorite things about
Sunday School.

Learning about Jesus

When I was just a baby,
Rock baby in arms.

I learned from Mom and Dad
Reach high.

How to eat and talk and hug.
Hug self.

This makes me very glad!
Clap.

Now that I am bigger,
Reach high.

I can learn of Jesus too.
Make sign of the cross.

I know that He loves all of us,
Hug self.

Me and you and you.
Point to self and others.

MUSIC
Sing "Jesus Loves the Little Children."

Jesus Knows My Name

I am a special child.
  Jesus knows my name.
    Point to self.

Even when I'm wild,
  He loves me all the same.
    Hug self.

The Holy Spirit called me
  To trust in God's own Son.
    Point up; cross hands over heart.

On the cross, He set me free
  And heavenly life has won.
    Make cross with fingers; point up.

SPIRITUAL DEVELOPMENT
Show Baptism mementos and talk about what happens at Baptism.

Church Manners

When I go to God's house, I do not stomp or shout.
I never slam the hymnbook. I never whine or pout.
  Walk in place; shake head no.

When I go to God's house, I try to think of others.
I do not bug my sisters, mama, papa, or my brothers.
  Walk in place; shake head no.

When I go to God's house, I'm careful what I do.
I draw on my own paper, not on hymnbooks or on pews.
  Walk in place; shake head no.

When I go to God's house, I'm careful what I say.
I always use my inside voice and bow my head to pray.
  Walk in place; bow head and fold hands.

ETIQUETTE
Discuss church manners. Practice using an inside voice by whispering a nursery rhyme.

God's House

When I go to God's house, I bow my head in prayer.
I thank God for this special place and all the gifts
   He shares.
     Walk in place; bow head and fold hands.

When I go to God's house, a joyful voice I raise.
I love to join God's people in singing hymns of praise.
     Walk in place; open hands like book and pretend to sing.

When I go to God's house, I'm sorry I've been bad.
I hear how Jesus died for me; then my heart is glad!
     Walk in place; make cross with fingers.

When I go to God's house, I stand on tippy-toes
To see the babies baptized like I was long ago.
     Walk in place; stand on tippy-toes.

When I go to God's house, Jesus talks to me.
I hear Him in the Bible; His blessings I receive.
     Walk in place; open hands like book.

When I go to God's house, my offering I give.
It helps to build God's kingdom so everyone may live.
     Walk in place; pretend to give an offering.

When I go to God's house, you can come along with me.
He has room for all of us; you're welcome as can be!
     Walk in place; beckon; spread arms wide.

ART
Make stained glass crosses. Precut black construction paper crosses. Color coffee filters with markers, and spray lightly with water. Dry. Glue crosses on filters and hang in windows.

I'm Sorry

Sometimes I hug
   and help and clap.
Sometimes I push
   and throw and slap.
     Clap; then pretend to push.

When I sin, I'm sorry
   and so sad.
I say, "God, forgive me
   when I'm bad."
     Draw tears on face; bow head and fold hands in prayer.

God says to me,
   "I love you so!
I forgive you,
   don't you know?
     Hug self; make sign of the cross.

"With My hands
   I will protect;
That's My promise;
   I won't forget."
     Hold hands palms up; shake head no.

MOVEMENT
Act out the actions described in the poem.

~~~~~~~~~~~~~~~~~~~~~~~~~~~~~~~~~~~
PRAYERS
~~~~~~~~~~~~~~~~~~~~~~~~~~~~~~~~~~~

Jesus Listens

I talk to Jesus here.
> *Point left.*

I talk to Jesus there.
> *Point right.*

I talk to Jesus everywhere.
> *Point as you move arm in half circle.*

I know He hears my prayers.
> *Point to ears.*

Sometimes He answers, "Yes."
> *Nod yes.*

Sometimes He answers, "No."
> *Shake head no.*

Sometimes He makes me wait awhile,
> *Hold up pointer finger.*

But He always hears my prayers.
> *Point to ears.*

MUSIC
Sing the words to the tune of "The Farmer in the Dell."

When I Pray

When I pray to God for help,
I know that He will hear.
> *Fold hands in prayer; point to ears.*

God listens to all my prayers,
And so I have no fear.
> *Fold hands in prayer; shake head no.*

When I pray to God with thanks,
I know that He will hear.
> *Fold hands in prayer; point to ears.*

God listens to all my prayers,
And so I have no fear.
> *Fold hands in prayer; shake head no.*

SPIRITUAL DEVELOPMENT
Pass around a small stuffed animal. When children get the animal, encourage them to "talk to God," offering a simple prayer request.

Thank-You Litany

Have children join you in saying the refrain from Psalm 107:1.

For apples and pumpkins and leaves that turn red,
Oh give thanks to the Lord, for He is good.
For snowmen and sledding and a nice warm bed,
Oh give thanks to the Lord, for He is good.
For tulips and robins and kites flying high,
Oh give thanks to the Lord, for He is good.
For sunshine and beaches and clouds in the sky,
Oh give thanks to the Lord, for He is good.
For eyes and ears and feet that run,
Oh give thanks to the Lord, for He is good.
But most of all for Jesus, God's Son—
Oh give thanks to the Lord, for He is good.

SCIENCE
Name the seasons, and discuss changes in them. Have children tell something about their favorite one.

Thank You, God

Thank You, God, for apple trees.
Extend arms like branches.

The crunchy apples taste so sweet!
Pretend to bite an apple.

Thank You, God, for loving me.
Hug self.

Thank You for these things I see . . .
Point to eyes.

Have children name things they see.

ORAL EXPRESSION
Have children name two other things they are thankful for.

Loving Hands

Give me loving hands to serve You—
Help me, dear Lord, I pray.
Hold hands, palms up; fold hands in prayer.

Show me how to use them
For You in every way. Amen.
Wiggle fingers; hold hands, palms up.

~~~~~~

CHURCH YEAR

~~~~~~

Church-Year Colors

Colors, colors, paint your story.
   Teach us of the Savior's glory!
Paint in air.

Advent Blue says, "Raise your eyes.
   He'll come back; look to the skies."
Look up, shading eyes with hand.

Christmas White says, "Jump for joy!
   Celebrate this baby boy!"
Jump.

Epiphany Green says, "See Jesus grow.
   We see Him revealed as God's Son,
you know."
Crouch down and grow up.

Lenten Purple says, "Let's pray,
   For forgiveness every day."
Bow head and fold hands.

Vivid Scarlet says, "Let's sing!
   On Palm Sunday, praise the King!"
Wave pretend palm branch.

Black Good Friday says, "A cross
   Was God's way to save the lost."
Make cross with fingers.

Easter White and Gold say, "See,
   An empty grave! He's set us free!"
Raise arms for freedom.

Pentecost Red says, "Go tell!"
   Jesus saves us; He makes us well."
Cup hands around mouth.

Colors, colors, paint your story.
   Teach us of the Savior's glory.
Paint in air.

LEARNING COLORS
Use nylon scarves or cut crepe-paper streamers to match the colors
named in the finger play. Have enough so each child gets one. When
children hear the color of their streamer, have them wave it in the air.

Advent

See the candles brightly glowing on the Advent wreath.
Wiggle fingers; make circle.

Soon the Savior will be born, born for you and me.
Rock baby in arms; point to others and self.

Light the candles, sing a song, wait and watch and pray.
Hold hands like book, pretending to sing; fold hands in prayer.

Soon the Savior will be born, born on Christmas Day.
Rock baby in arms; clap and smile.

Advent Counting

One, two, three, four—
Hold up fingers as you count.

It's hard to wait one week more.
Cross arms and tap toe.

Four, three, two, one—
Hold up four fingers, and put them down, one at a time.

Advent's waiting for God's Son.
Rock baby in arms.

COUNTING
Count the candles on the Advent wreath. Make a paper chain to count the days until Christmas.

Advent Waiting

In Advent we wait; in Advent we hope,
Tap toe; look up.

For the Savior God promised to send.
Open hands like Bible.

In Advent we wait; in Advent we hope,
Tap toe; look up.

For the King who is coming again.
Make crown on head with hands.

17

Christmas

Look and see. It's Bethlehem. Peek inside the stable.
Shade eyes with hand; bend down to peek in stable.

Look and see. It's Joseph. Come in, if you're able.
Shade eyes with hand; beckon.

Look and see. It's Mary there. She's become a mother.
Shade eyes with hand; point and nod head yes.

Look and see the Baby, swaddling cloths, His cover.
Shade eyes with hand; rock baby in arms.

Look and see. Who's visiting? Who's coming into view?
Shade eyes with hand; hold hands, palms up and shrug.

Look and see the shepherds, who heard the angel's news.
Shade eyes with hand; point to ears.

Look and see this Baby Boy. It's Jesus Christ, God's Son.
Shade eyes with hand; rock baby in arms.

Look and see the Savior. He's come for everyone.
Shade eyes with hand; point to others and to self.

VISUAL RECOGNITION
Point to or show the crèche and figures as you name each one.

Epiphany

Star light, star bright! Wise Men walking in the night.
Wiggle fingers; use fingers in a walking motion.

Star light, star bright! Lead us to the Savior's side.
Wiggle fingers; use fingers in a walking motion.

Star light, twinkling! Where's the Baby born a King?
Wiggle fingers; hold hands, palms up, in questioning gesture.

Star light, twinkling! See the gifts we have for Him.
Wiggle fingers; hold out hands to offer gifts.

Star light, star glow! Is this the Savior? Do you know?
Wiggle fingers; hold hands, palms up, in questioning gesture.

Star light, star glow! Yes, He'll save us from our foes.
Wiggle fingers; make cross with fingers.

MUSIC
Sing "We Three Kings." Have children think of what they would give Jesus.

Lent

In Lent, we remember that our sins cause pain
> *Look sad and pull corners of mouth down.*

And how Jesus went to the cross, our hearts to reclaim.
> *Cross hands over heart.*

Ask for forgiveness. His promise is true.
> *Fold hands in prayer.*

Our Jesus died for me and for you!
> *Point to self and others.*

FINE-MOTOR SKILLS
Cut purple crosses and put a smiley face on them.

Palm Sunday

Hosanna! Save us! Hosanna we cry.
> *Wave pretend palm branch.*

Hurry, hurry! King Jesus rides by.
> *Pretend to hold reins and ride a donkey.*

Hosanna! Save us! Hosanna we sing.
> *Wave pretend palm branch.*

He is our Savior. Let praises ring.
> *Pretend to ride donkey; wave palm branch.*

LANGUAGE/SOCIAL STUDIES
Have children list things they think of when they think of a king; for example, the color purple is a royal color.

Good Friday

Have children say the refrain.

On a cross upon a hill,
Jesus died for you and me.
> *Make cross with fingers; point to others, then self.*

With enemies and soldiers laughing,
Jesus died for you and me.
> *Make cross with fingers; point to others, then self.*

All according to God's plan,
Jesus died for you and me.
> *Make cross with fingers; point to others, then self.*

To take away all our sins,
Jesus died for you and me.
> *Make cross with fingers; point to others, then self.*

MUSIC
Sing "Do You Know Who Died for Me?"

19

Easter Day

Happy, happy Easter Day! This is what we want to say!
Wave arms back and forth; cup hands around mouth.

Jesus died for you and me, came back to life for all to see.
Make cross with fingers; point to eyes.

Happy, happy Easter Day. This is what we want to say!
Wave arms back and forth; cup hands around mouth.

FEELINGS
On paper plates, draw feelings such as happy, sad, angry, scared, and surprised. Have children name them and show the same feeling on their faces.

Ascension

Jesus told His disciples the things that they should do,
Point to mouth; nod head yes.

And all the things Jesus said are helpful for us too.
Point to mouth; hold hands, palms up.

He said to tell about His love to every boy and girl,
Point to mouth, then to children.

To each and every person all around the world.
Form circle with arms.

Then Jesus ascended to heaven; His time on earth was through.
Shade eyes and look up.

But He promises that He'll come back one day for me and you.
Nod head yes; point to self and others.

VOCABULARY
Make a list of words as you talk about what it means to "ascend" or ""go up": *rise, climb, mount, scale.*

Pentecost

On Pentecost, with fire and rushing wind—
Whoosh! The Holy Spirit came right in

Wiggle fingers over head for fire; sweep arm for "whoosh."

To give God's people power and might
To tell of Jesus, day and night.

Make a muscle; cup hands around mouth.

In us, the Holy Spirit also lives.
It's faith in Jesus that He gives.

Point to self; make cross with fingers.

He works in us so we may know:
God the Father loves us so.

Point to self; hug self.

SCIENCE
Talk about how we can see the effects of the wind, even though we can't see the wind itself. We can't see the Holy Spirit, but we can see what He does in the lives of God's children.

Holy Trinity

Three in One, Three in One,

Hold up 3 fingers, then 1.

God the Father and the Son

Hold up 1 finger, then 2 fingers.

And the Spirit, Three in One.

Hold up 3 fingers, then 1.

Our true God is Three in One.

Hold up 3 fingers, then 1.

MATH
Show things with three parts: sides of a triangle, leaves on a clover, petals on a trillium, parts of an apple (seeds, flesh, skin).

St. Michael and All Angels

On this day in September,
We give thanks and remember
Michael and all angels.

Fold hands; hook thumbs and flap like wings.

Shining bright with holy light,
Serving God with all their might,
Michael and all angels.

Hold hands out; hook thumbs and flap like wings.

Every night and every day,
Helping while we sleep or play,
Michael and all angels.

Rest head on hands; hook thumbs and flap like wings.

Bringing news of hope and love
From our Father up above,
Michael and all angels.

Point to sky; hook thumbs and flap like wings.

With their voices, we will raise
Prayers of thanks and songs
      of praise,
Michael and all angels.

Fold hands; hook thumbs and flap like wings.

MUSIC
Angels are God's helpers. They are around us even though we cannot see them. Sing "All Night, All Day, Angels Watching over Me."

Reformation Day

Martin Luther wrote one day
How the Church had lost its way.
Nailed that message on a door.
Tap, tap, tap, tap, tap.

Tap in rhythm to words.

"All you need is God's sweet grace,
Bible, Jesus, faith in place.
Those will open heaven's door."
Rap, rap, rap, rap, rap.

Knock in rhythm to words.

Celebrate what Luther said.
Wear your Reformation red
On October 31.
Clap, clap, clap, clap, clap.

Clap in rhythm to words.

MUSIC
March in place and sing words to the tune of "Row, Row, Row Your Boat."

All Saints' Day

Today is All Saints' Day—
A day the Church wears white.

Sweep arm in front of you; tug clothes for "wear."

It's the day we remember:
Jesus makes us perfect
   in God's sight!

Point to side of head; make cross with fingers.

Today is All Saints' Day—
We think of those in heav'n
   and on earth too.

Sweep arm in front of you; point to side of head.

It's the day we remember:
We are all God's saints—
   yes, even me and you!

Point to side of head; point to self and others.

ART
Write the word *Saint* followed by child's name in bubble letters. Have each child decorate his or her name.

~~~~~~

APOSTLES' CREED

~~~~~~

God the Father

God the Father, One in Three, is part of the Trinity.
With the Spirit and the Son, He is three, yet They are one.

Show 1 finger, then 3. Show 3 fingers, then 1.

God made everything you see: rainbows, clouds, and climbing trees.
He made every creature too; He made me, and He made you.

Shade eyes with hand. Point to others and to self.

Knows the hairs upon your head, hears your thoughts and things
   you've said.
That's because He's everywhere, keeps you safely in His care.

Point to ears and mouth. Sweep arm and hug self.

Food and things you need to live, all these things the Father gives.
He sent Jesus from above to be our Savior, out of love.

Pretend to eat. Make cross with fingers.

For such love, we cannot pay, so we're thankful and obey,
Till we enter heav'ns door, to live with Him forevermore.

Cross arms over chest. Point to sky.

LETTER RECOGNITION
Write *God* on board, then letter *G*. Review *g* sound. Children repeat words and stand when they hear "*g*" at the beginning of words you say; for example: go, hot, get, give, apple.

Jesus, God's Son

When I think of Jesus, my heart is filled with love.
He is my special friend, sent from God above.
Point up.

When I remember Jesus and think of Christmas morn,
I say, "Jesus is God's best gift. I'm glad that He was born!"
Clap.

When I think of Jesus, I know He lived for me.
He followed all God's rules, obeyed Him perfectly.
Nod head yes.

When I think of Jesus, I am so very glad.
He dries my tears and says, "I'm here when you are sad."
Wipe away pretend tears.

When I think of Jesus, and I've done something wrong,
I say, "Please, Lord, forgive me, and make my faith strong."
Make a muscle arm.

When I think of Jesus, I know that every day
He cares about my problems and listens when I pray.
Fold hands in prayer.

When I think of Jesus, I cry at what it cost.
He gladly gave His life for me and others on the cross.
Make cross with fingers.

When I think of Jesus, I know that I am saved.
I jump for joy! On Easter morn, there was an empty grave!
Jump.

When I think of Jesus with children on His knee,
I know He loves me deeply; there's always room for me.
Open arms.

When I think of Jesus, and I'm at heav'n's door,
He'll smile at me and gently say, "Come in; there's so
   much more!"
Beckon with arm; walk in place.

LETTER RECOGNITION
Write *Jesus* on board, then the letter *J*. Review the *j* sound. Children repeat words and stand when they hear *j* at the beginning of words you say; for example: joy, love, jar, jet, lion.

God the Holy Spirit

The Spirit makes me holy, bringing me to faith in Christ,
Blesses me and guides me, helps me lead a godly life.

Put hands over heart.

Came to me in Baptism, lives within me now each day,
Works a saving faith in me, helps me when I go astray.

Make sign of the cross.

Holy Spirit, You have called; in the Bible I have heard
How God loves me as His child, gives me faith by His own Word.

Open hands like book.

Holy Spirit, tongue of fire, help me tell about the cross.
Help me tell how Jesus saved us, how He seeks those who are lost.

Cup hands around mouth.

Holy Spirit always helping, gently whispers in my ear,
"To the Lord you are so special, God's own child so loved, so dear."

Hug self.

MUSIC
Sing a song about the Trinity, such as
"Father, I Adore You."

GOD'S CARE

God Is Good to Me

God is good to me. He gives me all I need.
Point up, then to self.

When I'm hungry, He gives me food.
Pat tummy with satisfied look.

When I'm sick, He helps me feel better.
Smile and skip.

When I'm scared, He helps me to be brave.
Make a muscle arm.

When I sin, He forgives me.
Make cross with fingers.

ART
Have children draw a picture of one of the statements.

God Is with Me

God is with me through the day,
When I sleep and when I play.
Put head on hands for sleeping; then jump.

He watches over all I do.
When troubles come, He's with me too.
Shade eyes with hand; hug self.

He does the same for you and you!
Thank You, God! I trust in You!
Point to others; put hands over heart.

God Cares for Me

God cares for me in the morning
When I hop out of my bed.

Hop in place.

God cares for me at playtime
When I'm running with my friends.

Run in place.

God cares for me at lunchtime
When I eat my food.

Pretend to eat.

God cares all through the nighttime.
My God is so good!

Put head on hands.

CRITICAL THINKING
Make a large clock with hands. Move the hands to different times of the day. Have children tell how God is with them and helps them at those times.

God Gives Me

God gives me
His Son, Jesus, who loves me.

Hug self.

God gives me
His forgiveness for Jesus' sake.

Make cross with fingers.

God gives me
People to love and care for me.

Point to others.

God gives me
His love to share.

Cross hands over chest, then hold them out.

LANGUAGE
Have children tell other things God gives them.

Jesus Loves Me

Jesus is so full of love.
He came to us from heaven above.

Hug self.

He healed the sick and cured the lame.
He gave all glory to God's name.

Point up.

He kept God's Law perfectly;
Then died on the cross for you and me.

Make cross with fingers.

Jesus loves us all so much, you see,
Now and for all eternity.

Hug self.

MUSIC
Sing "Jesus Loves Me, This I Know."

BIBLE WORDS

God's Word

The Bible is God's Word.
Open hands like book.

And every word is true.
Nod yes.

It tells me of God's love—
Hug self.

How He cares for me and you.
Point to self, then others.

I can learn some Bible words,
Point to head.

Just one or two each day.
Hold up 1, then 2, fingers.

Then I can tell others of Jesus.
Cup mouth.

I'll know just what to say.
Nod yes.

SPIRITUAL DEVELOPMENT
Have the children say Bible memory words to one another.

Here Is the Bible

Here is the Bible
God gave to me.
Open hands like book.

What does He tell me?
Let's look and see.
Shade eyes with hand.

Thank You, God

God helps the farmers when they sow.
Rain and sunshine make plants grow.

Wiggle fingers in downward motion; make big circle for sun.

Thank You, God, for everything.

Fold hands in prayer.

God gives us good food to eat.
God gives us juice that's, oh, so sweet.

Pretend to eat.

Thank You, God, for everything.

Fold hands in prayer.

The food will make our bodies strong
So we can have fun all day long.

Make a muscle arm; run in place.

Thank You, God, for everything.

Fold hands in prayer.

CRITICAL THINKING
Name your favorite foods.

Thank You for Our Food

All our food comes from God,

Point up.

Our juice and water too.

Pretend to drink.

For this yummy snack we say,

Pat tummy.

"Heavenly Father, thank You!"

Fold hands in prayer.

SPIRITUAL DEVELOPMENT
Pretend Jesus is having a snack with you; say a prayer.

Thanks

For food and drink and all we love,
Let's give thanks to God above.

Fold hands in prayer.

CREATIVE EXPRESSION
Draw a picture of your favorite food.

~~~~~~

GOING HOME

~~~~~~

Good-bye

Sunday School is over for another day.

Put hands out, palms up, then close them.

Now we're going home, happy as can be.

Walk in place.

We heard how God loves us and sent His only Son.

Point to ears.

Yes, Jesus came from heaven to die for you and me.

Point up, then to others and to self.

Now it's time to say good-bye

Point to mouth.

To each and every friend.

Point to others.

Wave to this one and to that one.

Wave.

Time for Sunday School to end.

Put hands out, palms up, then close them.

MATH
Count your Sunday School friends.

_____

Closing Prayer

Dear Jesus, You're my friend.
You love me every day.
Forgive me all my sins.
Help me to love, I pray.

Hug self; bow and fold hands in prayer.

I want to love my friends
And help them every day,
For they are gifts from You.
With love for them I pray:

Hug self; bow and fold hands in prayer.

Thank You, Jesus,
	for my friend(s): _____
Amen.

SPIRITUAL DEVELOPMENT
Invite children to name friends to pray for.

_____

Part 2
Bible Stories

God Creates the World

Genesis 1:1–2:3

God made the day, He made the night.
Put both hands up, then down.

God made the sun that shines so bright.
Make a big circle over head.

God made the earth, He made the seas.
Put both hands up, then down.

God made the flowers, plants, and trees.
Extend arms like branches.

God made the sharks, the fish, and whales.
Put hands together and move them back and forth like fish.

God made the peacock's lovely tail.
Fan hands out in front.

God made the hippos, dogs, and rats.
Point to pretend animals.

God made the zebras, gators, cats.
Point on each animal.

Creation looked just like it should.
Shade hand over eyes.

God was so happy; it was good!
Smile and clap.

CREATIVE EXPRESSION
Assign children a line of the poem to illustrate.
Write the words on the pictures and make an
illustrated book.

31

God Creates Adam and Eve

Genesis 1:26–2:25

God made the world. It all was good.
Make a big circle with arms.

When He spoke, some creatures stood!
Stand up tall.

But God formed something with His hands.
Show hands.

God took some clay and made a man!
Rub hands in circular motion as if creating.

God made that man with loving care.
Keep creating with hands.

Into that man God breathed some air.
Breathe in and blow out.

God named him Adam, gave him life.
Put hands on heart.

Decided next to make a wife.
Hold both hands out.

So God made Adam's helper and friend.
Hug self.

He named her Eve, and God loved them.
Put hands over heart.

BODY AWARENESS

Have children look in mirrors to see how special they are. Reinforce that God created each child and that each child is special! Talk about eyes, ears, mouths, and so forth, and the special task each has.

Sin Enters the World

Genesis 3

Have children point to ears, shake head no, and say the bold response.

There was a snake that came into the garden.
Don't listen to the snake! No, it's a big mistake!

The snake told Eve he had a bargain.
Don't listen to the snake! No, it's a big mistake!

The snake told Eve to eat fruit from God's tree.
Don't listen to the snake! No, it's a big mistake!

The snake told Eve the fruit would help her see.
Don't listen to the snake! No, it's a big mistake!

Eve knew it was wrong when she took that first bite.
Don't listen to the snake! No, it's a big mistake!

Then Eve gave some to Adam, who said, "All right."
Don't listen to the snake! No, it's a big mistake!

Now God knew He would have to send His Son.
Don't listen to the snake! No, it's a big mistake!

God would send Jesus to save everyone!

ART
Have children decorate crosses. Remind them of God's grace and amazing plan
to save all of His people.

Cain and Abel

Genesis 4:1–16

Two brothers brought their gifts, to offer to the Lord.
Abel thanked God with his heart; Cain used only words.
> *Cross hands over heart; point to mouth.*

God loved Abel's gift the best; this made Cain quite mad.
So Cain killed Abel in a field; this was very bad!
> *Pound fist on open palm.*

God knew what Cain had done and asked, "Where is your brother?"
Cain said, "I don't know where he is. I am not his mother!"
> *Put hands on hips; shake head no.*

Now God was sad and said, "Cain, you must go away."
But out of love, God put a mark on Cain to protect him on his way.
> *Write a letter in the air.*

Sometimes we are naughty too, in what we think and say and do.
But God loves us, and for Jesus' sake, He forgives both me and you.
> *Cross hands over heart; make cross with fingers.*

ORAL EXPRESSION
Describe gifts and talents we can give God and how God is pleased with our gifts because they are given in faith.

Noah and the Flood

Genesis 6:1–9:17

God was pleased with Noah, for he
believed in the Lord.
Hug self.

God told Noah, "Build an ark, and put
yourself onboard."
Point.

Noah and his family did what God told
them to do.
Nod head.

They worked to build the ark and got
ready for the zoo!
Hammer.

God sent two of every animal to get
aboard their boat.
Hold up 2 fingers.

He sent elephants and donkeys,
chimpanzees and goats.
Point on each animal you name.

Once everyone was loaded, and the ark
could fit no more.
Hold arms way out in front.

God Himself helped out Noah by
closing the ark's door!
Bang hands together.

The rain began and did not stop for
forty nights and days.
Hold hands, fingers down, and wiggle for rain.

But Noah's family and the animals
rocked safely on the waves.
Make waves with hands.

Finally the rain stopped, and down the
water went.
Lower hands to show waves receding.

The ark rested on a mountaintop;
Noah wondered what it meant.
Put hands up by shoulders, questioning.

Noah sent out a raven, then a dove or
two.
Link thumbs to make wings.

When the dove did not come back, it
was then that Noah knew.
Point to head.

Noah let out all the animals, and they
were glad to get away!
Point far away.

Then Noah and his family worshiped
God that very day.
Fold hands in prayer.

God promised Noah and his family, and
He promised you and me.
Point to others and to self.

There'd be no more big floods. Then He
gave His rainbow for all to see!
Make rainbow with hands.

SCIENCE
Have children pretend to be animals. Guess which animal.
Talk about rainbows and when they are seen in the sky.
What colors do they see?

Rainbow Hug

Genesis 9:12–15

A rainbow in the sky above
Form arch over head.

Tells us all of God's great love.
Cup hands around mouth.

It is a special gift you see—
Point to eyes.

God's promise hug for you and me.
Hug self.

Noah, Noah, What Do You See?

Genesis 7:8–9

Noah, Noah, what do you see?
I see my wife following me.
Wife, Wife, what do you see?
I see my son following me.
Son, Son, what do you see?
I see monkeys following me.
Monkeys, monkeys, what do you see?
I see tigers following me.
Tigers, tigers, what do you see?
I see rabbits following me.

Continue with other animals, ending with these words:

[Animals], [animals], what do you see?
I see children following me.
Children, children, what do you see?
I see God taking care of me!

VISUAL RECOGNITION
Select a child to be Noah. Have Noah choose the next
child and what character or animal the child will be. Have
children who are animals make animal sounds. Continue until
everyone has had a turn.

ABRAHAM AND ISAAC

God Calls Abraham

Genesis 12:1–9

God told Abraham, "Leave your home and country.
I will be with you and tell you where to go.
Point forward.

"I will bless you and make you a great nation."
Abraham obeyed God and left—he didn't say NO.
Shake head.

Abraham, Sarah, and Lot took all they owned
And traveled many miles over the hot sand.
Walk in place.

God was with them and guided them, day after day,
Until they came to Canaan—their new land. Hooray!
Clap.

CRITICAL THINKING
Ask, If you were going on a long trip, what would you take along?

Abraham Rescues Lot

Genesis 13—14

Abraham and Lot had so many animals,
There wasn't enough to feed them.
Shake head no.

"We need to move apart," said
Abraham.
So Lot went to live near Sodom.
Walk in place.

Enemies came to fight the king of
Sodom
And took Lot and his family away.
Make sad face.

So, Abraham gathered his fighting men
And went to rescue Lot that day.
Make a muscle arm; say hooray.

SOCIAL DEVELOPMENT
Ask, If you were Lot, how would you feel when the kings captured you? How would you feel when you were rescued?

God's Covenant with Abraham

Genesis 15:1–6; 17:15–27

Abraham and Sarah asked God for a son.
God made a promise to give them one.
> *Rock baby in arms.*

Their family would number like stars in the sky.
"Go ahead, count them," said God. "Just try."
> *Twinkle fingers; pretend to count stars.*

God gave Abraham faith that God's Word was true.
God gives us faith to trust in Him too.
> *Cross hands over heart.*

He sent Jesus to be our Savior and Friend.
Jesus' love lasts forever; it never ends!
> *Hug self.*

CREATIVE EXPRESSION
Make a picture of a starry sky by drawing lots of stars or using silver star stickers.

Abraham's Visitors from Heaven

Genesis 18:1–15

Three men came to see Abraham
> *Hold up 3 fingers.*

With some news he wanted to hear.
> *Point to ears.*

They spoke for God and told him this:
> *Point to mouth.*

"Sarah will have a son next year."
> *Rock baby in arms.*

When Sarah heard, she laughed and said,
> *Pretend to laugh.*

"I'm too old to have a baby!"
> *Rock baby in arms.*

But nothing is too hard for God.
> *Shake head no.*

He'll keep His promise. Wait and see.
> *Nod yes; point to eyes.*

MUSIC
Sing and act out "Father Abraham."

Abraham Believes

Hebrews 11:8–10

Abraham believed God's promises
Point up.

And knew that they were true.
Nod head.

We can believe God's promises
Point to self.

Because He loves me and you.
Hug self.

LANGUAGE DEVELOPMENT
Use the word *promise* during class (e.g., I promise to give you a snack;
I promise to give you a turn). Talk about God's promises.

The Birth of Isaac

Genesis 21:1–8

Abraham and Sarah wanted a son.
Rock baby in arms.

They waited and waited but still had none.
Hold hands, palms up, questioning.

Then God told Sarah she'd have a baby.
Rock baby in arms.

Sarah laughed out loud—she was an old lady.
Laugh.

But God's words were true, and the baby came.
Nod head yes.

Then Sarah said, "Isaac will be his name."
Rock baby in arms.

CRITICAL THINKING
Talk about names. Are the children named for a relative or a Bible person?
What does their name mean?

Abraham and Isaac

Genesis 22:1–19

"Abraham," said God, "I need something from you.
"Take Isaac, your son; this is what you should do."
   Shake pointer finger.

"I want you to offer this Isaac to Me."
Though hard, this dad trusted God's plan faithfully.
   Cross hands over heart.

Now God loved both Abraham and Isaac too.
This task was a test. What would Abraham do?
   Hold hands palms up, questioning.

Abraham laid Isaac on the altar that day.
Then God sent an angel to Abraham to say,
   Cup hands around mouth.

"Abraham, don't lay your hand on Isaac today.
I see you love God in the faith you display."
   Hold hand out in stop motion; smile broadly.

Then God sent a ram so the boy could go free.
God blessed Abraham for all people to see!
   Spread arms out in front of you.

SOUND RECOGNITION

Encourage children to listen for the sound
of the letters *a* and *i*. Brainstorm a list of
other words that start with long *a*'s and *i*'s.

Isaac and Rebekah

Genesis 24

One young Isaac living all alone
> *Hold up left pointer finger.*

Needed a wife to have and to hold.
> *Hold up right pointer finger.*

Which young girl would be just right
> *Shrug shoulders; hands out, palms up.*

To live with Isaac day and night?
> *Make sun with arms; put head on folded hands.*

Then Abraham's servant set off
to find
> *Walk in place.*

That one special girl God had
in mind.
> *Shade hands with eyes, searching.*

Was it Rebekah? Could she be
the one?
> *Hold up right pointer finger.*

The one God had chosen for
Abraham's son?
> *Hold up left pointer finger.*

She watered his camels and took
him to see
> *Imitate pouring water.*

Her daddy, who said, "Marry Isaac?
Feel free."
> *Hold hand out, palm up.*

He brought back Rebekah to be Isaac's
bride,
> *Walk in place.*

To live with him and work together,
side by side.
> *Hold up 2 pointer fingers.*

God blessed Abraham, the servant,
and then
> *Put hand on head.*

He blessed Isaac, too, with a wife
and a friend.
> *Hug self.*

For now one young Isaac was not
alone.
> *Hold up right pointer.*

He had one young Rebekah to share
his home.
> *Hold up left pointer finger; bring fingers together.*

MATH

Have children count the members of their family. Chart the class results. Talk about how God gives us moms and dads and other grown-ups to love us and care for us.

41

~~~~~~
JACOB'S STORY
~~~~~~

Jacob and Esau

Genesis 25:19–34; 27:1–40

Isaac and Rebekah had twin boys.
But the boys were not quite the same.

Shake head no.

One was hairy and one was smooth.
Esau and Jacob were their names.

Rub arms.

Now Isaac wanted to bless Esau,
For Isaac was old, blind, and sick.

Cover eyes.

Jacob heard Esau would be blessed
And decided to play a mean trick.

Rub hands together.

His mom helped Jacob put goatskins on,
Then she made Isaac's favorite meal.

Stir pot with hand.

Isaac said, "You don't sound like Esau!
Come closer, son, and let me feel!"

Rub arms.

So Isaac was tricked and blessed his son.
He gave Esau's gifts to Jacob that day!

Pretend to give gifts.

Jacob was happy, but Esau was mad!
So Jacob had to run far, far away!

Run in place.

CRITICAL THINKING

If you were going on a trip, think of how you would go (by car, airplane, boat, train, chariot, horse, wagon, bike, foot).

Jacob's Dream

Genesis 27:41–28:22

Jacob ran quickly a long, long, way;
Run in place.

Then down he lay at the end of the day.
Rest head on hands.

Up overhead in the heavens high,
Point up.

Many stars twinkled in the bright night sky.
Make twinkle fingers.

With a great big yawn, he closed his eyes to rest.
Rest head on hands.

And he dreamed a dream that was the best!
Hold thumbs up.

He saw a ladder and heavenly light
Pretend to climb ladder.

And many, many angels, shining bright.
Shield eyes from light.

And there at the top, why, there God sat!
Bow head.

God spoke to Jacob, and they did chat,
Point to mouth.

"This land is yours. I'll watch over you."
Hold hands out in front of you, palms up.

Jacob awoke with much to do.
Rub sleep from eyes.

He said, "I will follow God always."
Walk in place.

God kept His promise to Jacob that day,
Nod head yes.

And He keeps His promises to us too.
Point to self and others.

CREATIVE EXPRESSION
Have children draw a picture
of Jacob's dream.

The best was sending Jesus to save me and you!
Make cross with fingers.

Jacob's Family

Genesis 29:1–30:24

Jacob saw beautiful Rachel.
Shade eyes with hand, looking.

He wanted her for his wife.
Put hands over heart.

So Uncle Laban said, "Work first.
Put fist in palm.

Then start your new married life."
Spread hands out.

Jacob worked for seven long years,
Put fist in palm.

Yet the time went quickly by.
Point to wrist.

But Laban played a little trick;
Rub hands together.

That uncle told a big lie!
Use hands to show a big amount.

Leah was Rachel's big sister.
Use hand to go from low to high.

Jacob got Leah instead.
Cross hands in front of each other showing switching.

"But I worked for Rachel!"
Put fist in palm.

Said Jacob, scratching his head!
Scratch head, look confused.

"Work seven more years," said Laban.
Put fist in palm.

"And I will give her to you too."
Stretch out hands, offering gift.

So that is just what Jacob did.
Put fist in palm.

He didn't know what else to do.
Shrug shoulders.

God blessed Jacob's family.
Put hand on head in blessing.

He kept His promises to him.
Nod head yes.

God promises to bless us too!
Put hand on head in blessing.

Thank You, God! Thank You! Amen.
Fold hands in prayer.

MATH
Use manipulatives (blocks, buttons) to count out groups of seven or twelve.

God Gives Families

Genesis 29:1–30:24

God gave Jacob a family—
Leah, Rachel, and twelve sons.
God gave you a family too—
Can you name them, every one?

Have children name family members.

Esau Forgives Jacob

Genesis 31:3; 32:1–33:20

Esau was coming with 400 strong men!
Jacob was sorry, scared, and so sad.

March in place; hang head.

He didn't want to fight with his brother.
Jacob worried—was Esau still mad?

Put fists up; put arms up, questioning.

But Esau ran straight to his brother.
He gave him a hug and then cried,

Run in place; hug self.

"I forgive you, dear brother; I love you!"
The brothers stood, smiling, side by side.

Hug self; hold 2 pointer fingers together.

God wants us to love one another.
And for Jesus' sake, He forgives.

Hug self; make cross with fingers.

He helps us to follow His Word
And teaches us all how to live!

Open hands like book; nod yes.

DRAMATIC PLAY
Have children act out the story. Practice saying "I'm sorry" and "I forgive you."

JOSEPH AND HIS FAMILY

Joseph and His Brothers

Genesis 37

When Joseph was a lad, he had eleven brothers.
His father's name was Jacob; Rachel was his mother's.
Hold up 10 fingers and then 1.

Jacob pampered young Joseph because he loved him so,
Gave him a brightly colored coat that Joseph loved to show.
Pretend to show off coat.

When Joseph's brothers saw this, they said, "He's such a pest.
He thinks he's special just because our father likes him best."
Make mad face.

Then Joseph had a dream—the grain his brothers bound
Gathered all around his grain and bowed low to the ground.
Bow.

He had a second dream: eleven stars, the moon, and sun
Would each bow down to him, before the dream was done.
Bow.

"We'd never bow to you!" The brothers raged and ranted!
They planned to punish him and plotted how to get him.
Frowning, pound fist on palm.

FINE-MOTOR SKILLS
Practice zipping and buttoning by dressing up
in various coats.

Joseph's Troubles

Genesis 39

They got their chance when Joseph was away from Jacob's eye.
His brothers threw him in a pit till traders happened by.

Pretend to throw.

They took his coat and sold him off. "We're rid of him!" they said.
"Let's rip the coat and use it to tell Father that he's dead."

Pretend to rip coat.

Poor Joseph went to Egypt, where he worked hard for his master.
But still the Lord was with him, kept him safe from all disaster.

Hug self.

Still Joseph ended up in jail because a woman lied.
But even there he did good things, for God was on his side.

Pat self on shoulder.

This story is not over, for God had made great plans.
Soon He'd raise young Joseph up to be a mighty man.

Stand tall; make muscle.

In time, a famine hit the land, and when they had no food,
Joseph's brothers came to Egypt and got help from you-know-who!

Pretend to give food.

Through Joseph's brother Judah, God fulfilled His rescue plan.
One descendant was Christ Jesus, who delivers us from sin.

Make a cross with fingers.

MUSIC
When you get afraid of things, it helps to
sing and talk to God. Sing "God Is So Good."

Joseph Helps Pharaoh

Genesis 41

Pharaoh, king of Egypt, had a scary dream.
"Skinny cows ate fat cows; someone tell me what it means."

Move mouth as if chewing.

His wisest men were stumped, but a servant knew a name.
"Go get Joseph out of jail; with dreams he has some fame."

Shrug shoulders, palms up, puzzled; point to head for know.

"Your dreams, O King, mean bad times are coming Egypt's way.
So store up food right now, so you'll have plenty on that day."

Shake head no; pretend to pile up food.

The pharaoh was so thankful; he gave Joseph royal power
To store up food for all his kingdom in the coming hours.

Hold palms up, arms outstretched.

ART
Have children draw pictures to illustrate the story.

Joseph Forgives

Genesis 42–45

There was no food in all their land, so Joseph's band of brothers
Went to Egypt and begged Joseph for food for all the others.

Bow with hands out.

Joseph knew who they were, but they did not know him.
So he tested them before he filled their baskets to the brim.

Look surprised.

When he told his brothers "I'm Joseph" with a tear,
They knew that they were guilty and began to shake with fear.

Shake with fear.

"The bad things that you did," he said, "God has turned to good.
I forgive you now; let's live in peace like families should."

Pat head.

SPIRITUAL DEVELOPMENT
List ways to show love in a family. Pray for forgiveness for the times
we do not show love in our families.

~~~~~~

MOSES AND THE EXODUS

~~~~~~

The Birth of Moses

Exodus 1:1–2:10

"Take all the baby boys," said Pharaoh,
"Into the river they must go!"
Pretend to throw.

The Hebrew women were so sad.
One baby's mom shook her head no.
Hold hands on hips and shake head.

She put her baby in a basket.
Down the river he began to float.
Make waves with hands.

His big sister watched over his travels.
His basket was like a little boat!
Cup hands for boat.

Pharaoh's daughter was surprised
To see a little basket float near.
Make waves with hands.

When she opened it, she cried,
"Why, there's a baby in here!"
Rock baby in arms.

God kept baby Moses safe
Because God had a plan, you see!
Point to eyes.

God was going to use Moses
To set God's people free!
Stretch hands out wide.

SCIENCE

Use a tub of water for water exploration. Set out cups, containers, and pumps to move the water to see what sinks and what floats. Have children make predictions; then observe what happens.

Moses and the Burning Bush

Exodus 2:11–4:31

Moses grew up and left Egypt.
Now his job was herding sheep.

Walk in place holding a pretend staff.

One day he was watching his flock,
When something made his heart leap!

Put hands on cheeks.

Moses saw a bush that was on fire.
But the branches and leaves were fine.

Hold up arms like branches.

Then he heard a voice from the bush,
"Moses, come here. You are Mine."

Beckon with arm.

"I am the Lord," said the voice.
"I have a new job for you.

Point.

You will free My people from Pharaoh.
That is what you must do!"

Nod head.

So Moses listened to God.
And Aaron, his brother, came too.

Beckon with arm.

God was with them as they went.
God showed them what to do.

Point outward.

LANGUAGE DEVELOPMENT
Have children sit in a circle and play telephone. Begin by whispering "Moses" or "Jesus loves you" in ear of first child. Have that child whisper word or phrase to next child and so on. (It's okay if children hear it from other children.) The activity helps them practice vocal volume control and listening skills.

51

Moses and the Plagues

Exodus 5–10

Moses went to Pharaoh;
Walk in place.

"God says, 'Let My people go.'"
Point outward.

God turned the Nile to blood.
Make waves like river.

But the pharaoh still said, "No!"
Shake head no.

Moses went to Pharaoh;
Walk in place.

"God says, 'Let My people go.'"
Point outward.

God sent frogs hopping.
Hop.

But the pharaoh still said, "No!"
Shake head no.

Moses went to Pharaoh;
Walk in place.

"God says, 'Let My people go.'"
Point outward.

God sent millions of gnats to bite.
Swat bugs off arms.

But the pharaoh still said, "No!"
Shake head no.

Moses went to Pharaoh;
Walk in place.

"God says, 'Let My people go.'"
Point outward.

God sent swarms of flies.
Swat hands in front of face.

But the pharaoh still said, "No!"
Shake head no.

Moses went to Pharaoh,
Walk in place.

"God says, 'Let My people go.'"
Point outward.

God made the cows die.
Hold head sideways.

But the pharaoh still said, "No!"
Shake head no.

Moses went to Pharaoh;
Walk in place.

"God says, 'Let My people go.'"
Point outward.

God sent sores to the Egyptians.
Pick at arms.

But the pharaoh still said, "No!"
Shake head no.

Moses went to Pharaoh;

Walk in place.

"God says, 'Let My people go.'"

Point outward.

God sent hail to beat the crops.

Move hands, palms down, up and down.

But the pharaoh still said, "No!"

Shake head no.

Moses went to Pharaoh;

Walk in place.

"God says, 'Let My people go.'"

Point outward.

God sent locusts to eat the food.

Put hands by mouth chewing.

But the pharaoh still said, "No!"

Shake head no.

Moses went to Pharaoh;

Walk in place.

"God says, 'Let My people go.'"

Point outward.

God covered the land in darkness.

Cover eyes.

But the pharaoh still said, "No!"

Shake head no.

LITERATURE

Have children draw pictures to illustrate each plague. Write the words from the finger play on the corresponding picture. Bind pages together into a classroom book.

The Passover

Exodus 11—12

God was tired of Pharaoh's answer.
It was time for Pharaoh to be done.
Swipe hands back and forth.

So God sent His angel of death
To claim the firstborn sons.
Hold arms out for angel.

But the children of God were safe.
For they listened to what God had to say.
Point to ears.

They took the blood of a lamb,
And painted their doorposts that day.
Pretend to paint.

The angel of death passed over
The doorposts that were painted red.
Pretend to paint.

But the Egyptians who did not believe
Woke up to find their firstborn sons
  dead.
Pretend to rub sleep from eyes.

The children of God were packed and
  ready.
They had prayed for this day long ago.
Fold hands in prayer.

This time when Moses asked Pharaoh,
Pharaoh said, "Take your people and go!"
Cheer!

CRITICAL THINKING

Pass around a small suitcase or duffel bag. Invite children to pretend they are going on a trip. When children get the bag, say, "I am going on a trip. Jesus is with me when I go to (name of place)." Have child fill in the name and say how he or she will get there (e.g., by car, train, plane) or what he or she might see along the way.

Crossing the Red Sea

Exodus 13:17–15:21

Grumble, grumble. Where can we go?
Look left and right

Pharaoh's army is coming fast—oh, no!
Run in place quickly, then slowly.

Water on one side; mountains, the other.
Look side to side.

We should go back—this is a bother!
Point over shoulder.

But Moses said, "God is with us; you'll see."
Point up.

Then the wind blew, and God parted the sea!
Blow like wind.

God's people walked quickly to the other side.
Walk in place.

The Egyptian soldiers and chariots also tried.
Walk in place.

But before they could make it, their wheels got stuck.
Walk in place as if stuck in mud.

Then the waters returned and gobbled them up!
Cover head with arms.

God saved all His people! He cares, it's true,
Nod head yes.

For His people Israel and for me and for you!
Give high fives.

GROSS-MOTOR SKILLS
Make a path on the floor with two strips of masking tape. Challenge the children to "go through the Red Sea" in as many different ways as they can (e.g., hopping, jumping, skipping, crawling, taking baby steps or giant steps).

ISRAEL IN THE WILDERNESS

God Provides Manna and Quail

Exodus 16–17

Moses led God's Hebrew band, as they walked through desert sand.
Stomachs rumbled, so they grumbled. Trudge, trudge, trudge.
> *Rub stomachs, walk in place.*

"When in Egypt we could dine every day on food so fine,
Moses, heed us! Who will feed us?" Trudge, trudge, trudge.
> *Pretend to eat.*

So in evening without fail, God would send them scads of quail.
Also, heavenly bread was found every morning on the ground.
> *Pretend to pick up things from ground.*

God said, "This you must obey; eat My bread within a day.
If you don't, it will get germy, rotten, foul, and even wormy."
> *Make sour face.*

Thus the Lord, for forty years, answered all His people's fears,
Kept them safe through desert sand, till they reached the Promised Land.
> *Hug self.*

SCIENCE
Desert plants must live on little water. Show cacti and talk about why we don't touch them.

The Ten Commandments

Exodus 19–20

Moses went up Mount Sinai, just as God told him to do.
God gave him Ten Commandments, laws for living good and true.
Pretend to hike up mountain.

Have no other gods, but Me; it's My love that sets you free.
Point finger to sky in one-way sign.

Use My name for prayer and praise, only in respectful ways.
Bow head.

Keep the Sabbath Day apart; worship Me with all your heart.
Cross hands over heart.

Honor parents with your love. They're a gift from up above.
Point up.

Do not kill or hurt each other; treat all kindly like a brother.
Look mad; then smile.

Husbands, wives, show love each day—faithful, loyal, never stray.
Clasp hands.

Do not steal things old or new, for they don't belong to you.
Put hands behind back.

Help your neighbors; don't tell lies; lift them up in others' eyes.
Put hand over mouth.

Do not covet your neighbor's house, workers, animals, or spouse.
Shake head no.

SOCIAL SCIENCE
Rules keep us safe. Have children name one rule at home or school and how it keeps us safe.

Worship in the Tabernacle

Exodus 40

God told Moses, "Make My house
   a Tabernacle Tent.
Fill it with My holy things,
   then worship and repent.
   Put tips of fingers together to make tent.

In My Tabernacle Tent,
   My blessings you'll receive.
You are the people that I love,
   and I will never leave.
   Pat head.

I'll place a cloud above it,
   so watch it with your eyes.
Pack your things and follow,
   as it moves across the skies.
   Shade eyes with hand.

In my Tabernacle Tent,
   My glory you shall see.
My mercy and salvation
   through all eternity."
   Make cross with fingers.

SPIRITUAL DEVELOPMENT
Use a parachute or sheets as a tent; have Jesus
Time under it.

The Twelve Spies in Canaan

Numbers 13–14

The Lord said, "Moses, Moses, send
   twelve spies.
They will be your ears and eyes.
Send them to the Canaan land.
I will put it in your hand."
   Point to ears and eyes.

Two spies said, "Wow, this Canaan
   land is sweet!
God will lay it at our feet.
Grapes so big that it takes two
Just to bring them back to you!"
   Pretend to hold something heavy.

Ten spies said, "They have cities
   with great walls.
They are huge, while we are small.
They will not be giving hugs.
They will squash us like we're bugs!"
   Pretend to step on bug.

The Lord said, "You have doubts, and
   you have fears.
Now you'll wander forty years!
When you learn to trust in Me,
Then the Promised Land you'll see."
   Shake pointer finger.

SPIRITUAL/LETTER RECOGNITION
"T/t" is for trust. Make a capital *T* with fingers and a
lowercase *t* with fingers. What does the lowercase *t*
look like? A cross. *T* is for trust in Jesus.

The Bronze Serpent

Numbers 21:4–9

The people came to Moses, and they began to bleat,
"We hate this water and this food you've given us to eat!
Frown, and put hands on hips.

Oh, why did we leave Egypt? At least while we were there,
The food and water given us were pretty decent fare."
Hold elbows to side, palms up, eyes up.

The Lord sent snakes among them—one bite made people die—
To remind them to be thankful and trust in God on high.
Wiggle arms and hands like snakes; point up for "God."

"Moses, we have sinned against you and against the Lord.
Please forgive us and please save us from this snaky horde!"
Clasp hands, pleading.

"Make a snake of bronze," said God, "on a pole to hold it high.
If you're bitten, look at it, and then you will not die."
Shade eyes with hand, looking up.

Those who looked upon the pole recovered from the bites.
Then they were thankful to our God, both day and night.
Fold hands in prayer.

Another pole was lifted high, our Jesus on the cross.
All who put their trust in Him shall live and not be lost.
Make cross with fingers; cross hands over heart.

SCIENCE
Show pictures of snakes. Snakes belong to the animal group "reptiles" along with turtles, lizards, alligators, and crocodiles. Tell children, "Snakes are covered in scales, not feathers or fur. Do not pick them up because they can bite. Tell your parents if you find a snake."

~~~~~~

ISRAEL IN THE PROMISED LAND

~~~~~~

Crossing the Jordan

Joshua 3:3–5:12

Joshua listened to the Lord; he did as God said.

> *Point to ears.*

Carrying the ark of the covenant, the priests moved ahead.

> *Walk in place.*

Then the people behind, from every tribe,

> *Wiggle all 10 fingers.*

Crossed over the Jordan to the other side.

> *Walk in place.*

Twelve men each took a stone so no one would forget

> *Point to head.*

How the waters stood still, so they wouldn't get wet!

> *Shake head.*

Then the priests brought the ark of the covenant up safe,

> *Make thumbs-up.*

And the waters returned and flowed in their place.

> *Make a wave motion.*

MATH

Count rocks or stones. With smaller stones, try piling twelve together.

The Fall of Jericho

Joshua 6

God said, "Take seven priests with trumpets
Hold up 7 fingers.

And make a great rumble.
Cover ears.

On day 7, with shouts and trumpets,
Cup hands by mouth.

The walls will tumble."
Roll hands.

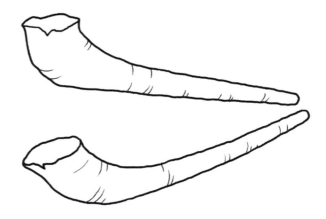

Day 1—once around Jericho.
Hold up 1 finger; move it in circular motion.

Day 2—once around Jericho.
Hold up 2 fingers; move them in circular motion.

Day 3—once around Jericho.
Hold up 3 fingers; move them in circular motion.

Day 4—once around Jericho.
Hold up 4 fingers; move them in circular motion.

Day 5—once around Jericho.
Hold up 5 fingers; move them in circular motion.

Day 6—once around Jericho.
Hold up 6 fingers; move them in circular motion.

Day 7—once around, twice around,
Three, four, five times around,
Hold up 1, 2, 3, 4, 5 fingers.

Six and then seven!
Hold up 6 and then 7 fingers.

Lifting trumpets toward heaven.
Pretend to blow trumpet.

With trumpets and shouts,
Cup hands by mouth.

They made a great rumble.
Cover ears.

And the walls of Jericho
Make a square for walls.

Crumbled and tumbled!
Roll hands.

God loves His people.
Hug self.

He loves us too.
Point to self and others.

In faith, we can trust Him
Cross hands over chest.

In all that we do.
Sweep hands out.

SCIENCE
Explore tuning forks and other types of vibrations.

Deborah

Judges 4–5

Deborah was a judge, wise and good.
Point to head and nod.

She helped God's people do as they should.
Make thumbs-up.

One day she called General Barak to her side.
Cup hands around mouth.

She said, "Get your men and be ready to ride.
Pretend to ride.

God's people need help—you must go to their aid."
Point on "you."

But Barak would not go, for he was afraid.
Tremble.

Then he said he'd go if Deborah went too.
Point back and forth to self and away.

So she did, because that's what God wanted them to do!
Nod head.

God's people succeeded— the victory was won!
Make a V for victory.

God had chosen Deborah to get the job done.
Shout hooray.

SOCIAL/EMOTIONAL DEVELOPMENT
Talk about fear. Ask, What makes you afraid?
New places, strange places, new things to
do? God takes care of you!

Gideon

Judges 6:11–7:25

The grain was stolen by enemies.
Make sad face.

The people prayed, "O God, help us please!"
Fold hands.

God was with Gideon and told him what to do.
Point; nod head yes.

Gideon blew a horn, long and loud.
Pretend to blow horn.

Many soldiers came—a great big crowd.
Spread arms wide.

God said, "Too many soldiers; this isn't right.
Shake head no.

Send home everyone who's afraid to fight.
Look scared.

Still too many men to do what I planned.
Shake head.

Take only the men that drink from their hand."
Drink.

God was with Gideon and told him what to do.
Point up, then nod head.

Three hundred men were left to fight the war.
Pretend to box.

Each man had a horn and a torch in a jar.
Pretend to blow horn.

The enemies were sleeping when the men came.
Lay head on hands.

They blew their horns and showed the torches' flame.
Blow.

The enemies awoke in the dark, black night.
Rub eyes.

They were so scared, they ran away in fright.
Run in place.

God was with Gideon and told him what to do.
Point up; nod head yes.

DRAMATIC PLAY
Review the Bible story by having the children do the actions that go with the rhyme.

Samson

Judges 16

"Samson, I'll make you very strong," God said.
Make a muscle.

"But you mustn't cut the hair on your head."
Point to head.

Samson's secret was revealed to his enemy.
Look mean.

They cut his hair! Now he was weak as he could be.
Make cutting motion.

Samson ended up in jail, and his hair began to grow.
Point to hair.

"I'm sorry, Lord," he prayed. "Please forgive me now."
Fold hands in prayer.

God heard his prayer and made him strong once more.
Make a muscle.

Samson pushed two pillars, and the roof crashed to
the floor!
Push.

Strong Samson had saved God's people from their
enemy.
Make a muscle.

Jesus is much stronger—
He saves us eternally!
Cross arms over chest.

SPIRITUAL DEVELOPMENT
How does Jesus love and save you?

Ruth

The Book of Ruth

Ruth said to Naomi,
    "I will stay with you."
Point to self, then someone else.

They were too poor to buy any food.
    Look sad.

Ruth said, "I will gather grain for you."
    Point to self, then someone else.

Ruth gathered some grain in Boaz's field.
    Gather grain.

Boaz said to Ruth,
    "You are very loving and kind."
    Smile.

Boaz loved Ruth, and he married her.
    Hug self.

Boaz said to Naomi,
    "Live with us; we don't mind."
    Smile and beckon with arm.

SOCIAL/EMOTIONAL DEVELOPMENT
Have children name a way they can show love to the people in their family.

God's Servant Samuel

1 Samuel 1–3

When Samuel was a little boy,
    his mother took him to
Live with Eli, God's own priest,
    and serve the Lord so true.
    Hold hands out to serve.

One night when he was sleeping,
    he heard his name so clear.
He ran to Eli's bedside; then he said,
    "Eli, I am here."
    Run in place.

But Eli had not called him.
    Then it happened twice again.
Eli said, "It's God you're hearing.
    Say you're listening."
    Point to ears.

From that day on, Samuel served
    God's people with great love
By telling them God's messages,
    sent down from heav'n above.
    Point to heaven and then to people.

SCIENCE
Have children stay quiet for a minute and listen. Then have them tell everything they heard in that minute.

Saul Becomes King

1 Samuel 8–10; 11:12–15

God's people looked around them and noticed several things,
The others living near them had some leaders they called kings.
Look around.

The people said to Samuel, "We want a king that's swell,
Someone that we can follow, so do the choosing well."
Make crown on head.

"Be careful what you wish for," the Lord Almighty said.
"Kings start wars and cost a lot; it's part of being led."
Shake finger.

But did the people listen? They said, "We know what's best!"
So God told Samuel, "I shall pick a king to lead the rest."
Cover ears.

A man named Saul was searching for donkeys one fine day.
He was tall and very strong and had a kingly way.
Stand tall; look kingly.

He ran right into Samuel, who said, "God has a plan.
God has chosen you for king! Yes, you shall be God's man.
Point.

"I'll pour some oil on you, so bow your head and kneel.
You'll serve the Lord Almighty, as king of Israel!"
Kneel and bow head.

MATH
Boys are called kings; girls are called queens. Graph how many kings and queens are in your room.

David and Goliath

1 Samuel 17

The Philistines were fighting the army of King Saul.
They were enemies of God and planned to take it all.
Pretend to shoot arrow.

A giant named Goliath shouted to Saul's men,
"Send a fighter to me, and we'll see which one can win.
Cup mouth with hands like shouting.

If I win, we'll be your slaves; I lose, and we are yours.
But first you have to beat me, and that is quite a chore."
Pound fist in open hand.

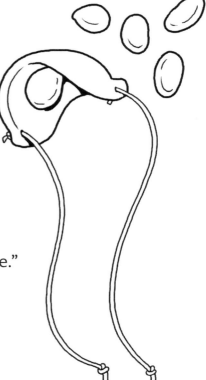

To face Goliath in a fight caused men to shake with fear,
So David stepped up to the front and said, "I volunteer."
Shake with fear.

"No," said Saul. "You're young and small. Just let the matter be."
"I can beat him," David said, "for God will be with me."
Point to sky.

"David, take my armor," Saul said. "Go and fight in it."
David said, "No thanks. This armor's heavy and won't fit."
Squat like being pushed down.

David picked up five round stones from in the riverbed.
He hurled one in his sling and smacked the giant in the head!
Pretend to throw stone.

"We won!" Saul's army shouted. "We'll never have to hide!
Even giants tumble when the Lord is on our side!"
Jump and clap.

GROSS-MOTOR SKILLS
Use tennis balls and cones. Place a cone as a target. Throw ball beyond the cone. Keep increasing the distance.

David and Jonathan

1 Samuel 18:1–5; 20:1–42

David loved to play his harp and praise God every day.
Saul so loved the music that he asked David to stay.
> *Pretend to play harp.*

It can be quite lonely to leave your mom and dad.
Being in a strange place with no friends can even make you sad.
> *Draw tears on face.*

But God sent David a good friend; he was one of Saul's sons.
They liked each other from the start. His name was Jonathan.
> *Smile.*

Jonathan gave David gifts—his bow, belt, robe, and sword.
"I pledge my help and friendship here to you before the Lord."
> *Open hands, palms up, offering gifts.*

Jonathan warned David when Saul began to crack.
He kept David safe when Saul would go on the attack.
> *Put fingers to lips and say "Shhh."*

So if you have some good friends, be sure to stop and pray,
"Thank You, Father, for my friends who brighten up my day."
> *Fold hands in prayer.*

SPIRITUAL DEVELOPMENT
Have children draw a picture of one friend and tell one fun thing they do together. Pray for that friend.

David Becomes King

1 Samuel 16:1–13; 2 Samuel 5:1–10

For a while Saul did fine, but then he acted odd,
Started doing naughty things and disobeying God.
Frown; shake finger.

God needs a new king, another chosen one.
Samuel went to Bethlehem, looked over Jesse's sons.
Put hand over eyes, searching.

"Do you have another?" Samuel asked the dad.
"Yes, I do," said Jesse, "but he is just a lad."
Shrug shoulders, palms up.

"My youngest son, named David, cares for my sheep and lambs.
Do you think that God would pick someone young like him?"
Look to sky with questioning look.

God said, "I pick David," and made the shepherd, king.
Together they would lead God's people and do wond'rous things.
Point finger.

SOCIAL DEVELOPMENT
Play follow the leader for several days, letting each child lead. Point out that good leaders think of others.

Nathan and David

2 Samuel 12:1–23

David was a good king, a man of God's own heart.
He loved the Lord and tried to follow God's rules from the start.
Put hand over heart.

But David took some things that were not his to take.
So God said, "David, what you did has caused My heart to break."
Put fists together and then pull apart.

At first David would not admit to God just what he had done,
But God sent Prophet Nathan, who wouldn't let him run.
Fold arms and frown.

"I'm sorry, Lord," said David. "Please make my spirit new.
Please help me walk with You again and do what I must do."
Bow head; fold hands.

God still loved King David, yet sin can have a cost—
David's house had trouble; the peace within was lost.
Draw tears on face with fingers.

We, too, can go astray from what God says to do.
In faith, we know He loves us and, in Christ, forgives us too.
Clap hands and smile.

SOCIAL DEVELOPMENT
List ways we bug each other—touching, taking stuff, not letting others play. Practice saying, "I'm sorry. Please forgive me."

Solomon Builds the Temple

1 Kings 5–6

Thousands of men are working hard—
  Work, work, work.
Pretend to hammer.

They chop down cedar and pine trees—
  Chop, chop, chop.
Pretend to chop.

They cut out huge chunks of stone—
  Cut, cut, cut.
Use fingers to make cutting motion.

Solomon is building a temple for God.

The temple is three stories high—
  High, high, high.
Use hand to show high, higher, highest.

Walls are carved with fruit and flowers—
  Carve, carve, carve.
Pretend to carve.

Rooms and altars are covered with gold—
  Cover, cover, cover.
Cover head with hands.

Solomon is building a temple for God.

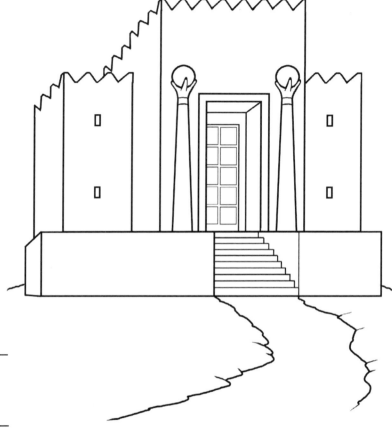

LANGUAGE DEVELOPMENT
Describe some of the furnishings in your church.

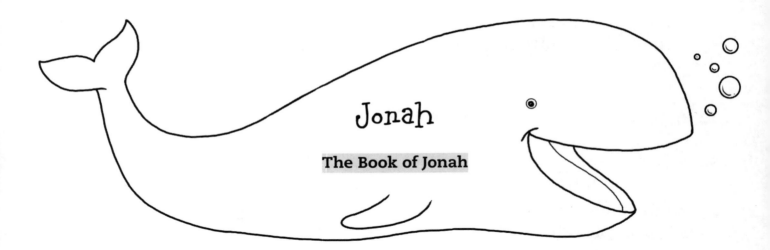

Jonah

The Book of Jonah

God told Jonah, "Go to Nineveh.
Point forward.

Tell the people all about Me."
Point up.

But Jonah went the other way.
Turn around.

He hopped on a ship and sailed
out to sea!
Hop.

A big storm made the waves
splash high.
Make a wave motion.

It seemed the ship would break apart.
Wring hands.

The sailors were afraid they'd die
Look scared.

Because of Jonah's disobedient heart.
Point to heart.

Jonah cried, "Just toss me overboard."
Use hand to make a diving motion.

Then down into the waves he went.
Make a wave motion.

His rescue had been planned
by the Lord.
Point up.

Gulp! A big fish caught him—
one God sent!
Open and shut hands like a mouth.

Inside the fish, sorry Jonah prayed.
Fold hands.

God sent the fish to some sand.
Wriggle hands like fish.

It spit out Jonah, who now obeyed
Move hand in an arc.

And told of God's love through
all the land!
Walk in place.

CREATIVE EXPRESSION
Make a picture of part of the story.

King Hezekiah Prays

2 Kings 18–19

Many, many years ago,
There was a king who loved God so.
Make crown over head.

King Hezekiah was his name.
He led God's people to do the same.
Nod head yes.

But a bad king sent soldiers from town to town
To steal and fight and tear things down.
Make a fist.

When King Hezekiah heard what they did,
He went to the church and bowed his head.
Bow head.

"Dear God," he prayed, "These men make fun of You.
Please save Your people and show us what to do."
Fold hands.

God heard King Hezekiah's prayer to Him.
Isaiah came to the king's servants to talk with them:
Walk fingers.

"Tell Hezekiah don't be afraid of what he hears and sees.
God has heard his prayer and will set His people free."
Fold hands.

That night an angel came to fight the bad men with His hand.
The other soldiers ran away and went back to their own land.
Run in place.

Now there were no enemy soldiers left to fight.
God saved His people with His great love and might!
Cross arms over chest.

SPIRITUAL DEVELOPMENT
Have a guest share stories of how God has answered his or her prayers.

ELIJAH AND ELISHA

God Cares for Elijah

1 Kings 17

Ahab was now king, and things weren't going well.
Ahab bowed to idols, not to the God of Israel.
Make crown with fingers on head; bow.

Elijah was God's prophet; God sent him to the king:
"God is mad at you because you worship other things.
Frown, shake finger.

God will not send rain; the crops will die away.
The people will go hungry, each and every day."
Rub stomach.

King Ahab got so mad, Elijah had to hide.
God sent him to the desert but stayed right by his side.
Pretend to hide.

God sent birds to feed him, so he would not get weak.
Each day and night the meat and bread were carried in their beaks.
Use hands like beaks.

Next God sent Elijah to a widow and her son.
They were eating their last meal, barely food for one.
Rub stomach.

"God will keep on feeding us," Elijah said. "Trust Him."
And God did, for every day the food jars filled again.
Smile, eat.

Like Elijah, we are fed by God in heav'n above.
He gives us everything we need; in Jesus, shows
    His love.
Hand on heart.

CRITICAL THINKING
Use plastic food, water, warm jackets, toys, books, and other items.
Sort into needs and wants.

Elijah and the Prophets of Baal

1 Kings 18:20–46

King Ahab bowed to idols, worshiped one called Baal.
He prayed for rain, but no rain came, and so the crops did fail.
> *Make crown with fingers on head; bow.*

Elijah said, "Let's test your god. I think you will be shocked.
Your god has no real power; he's only made of rock."
> *Put hands on sides of face; make muscle arm.*

The followers of Baal built an altar of their own.
Elijah also built the Lord an altar made of stone.
> *Pretend to build with stones.*

When Baal did not send fire, as his followers prayed,
Elijah teased them, saying, "Maybe Baal's not here today."
> *Cover mouth with hand and laugh.*

Then God sent flames from heav'n, so hot and blazing high,
The altar stones were turned to ash, and black smoke filled the sky.
> *Wipe brow and fan self; point up.*

The people said, "That Baal's a fake. Let's worship the true God."
A short time later, God sent rain, and God's people then had food.
> *Cross hands over chest and bow head; twinkle fingers like rain falling.*

HEALTH/COMMUNITY
Arrange for someone from the fire department to visit and give an age-appropriate fire safety lesson.

God Takes Elijah to Heaven

2 Kings 2:1–15

God picked Eli-JAH's helper, a man who worked a plow.
"Eli-SHA, travel with this prophet; follow now."
Push plow.

They told the people of God's love and taught them of God's heart.
Eli-JAH did some wond'rous things like make a river part.
Hold hands together, then push apart.

Eli-JAH asked Eli-SHA, "What can I do for you?"
Eli-SHA said, "Give me the spirit God gave you—times two."
Hold up 2 fingers.

Just then a chariot of fire streaked
     flaming through the sky,
Whisked Eli-JAH straight to heaven
     to live with God on high.
Look up with surprise on face and point.

Eli-JAH's coat fell to the ground; this
     sign from God said yes.
Eli-SHA would be a prophet too, and
     all the people he would bless.
Put hand on head in blessing.

SPIRITUAL DEVELOPMENT
Take children on a walk and have them look for things that make them think of heaven (e.g., a beautiful stained glass window, a cross for Jesus, the joy of people laughing, good food).

Hooray for E!

2 Kings 2:1–12

E is for Elijah,
God's man of long ago.
God took him home to heaven
In a chariot, long and low.

E is found in Easter,
The day Jesus said, "I'm here.
I died, but I'm alive again
For you, My friends, so dear."

E is at the end of me.
A little word, it's true.
But who does God want to live with Him?
I know—it's me and you!

LANGUAGE DEVELOPMENT
Have children say this refrain at the end of each verse: "Hooray for E! Hooray for E! A special letter for you and me."

Naaman and Elisha

2 Kings 5:1–14

Naaman was a mighty man, a warrior of great pride.
But now he had a skin disease that made him sad inside.
Pretend to cry.

A servant girl from Israel said, "I think I know a man—
The prophet from my country could heal poor Naaman."
Tap head with finger.

Naaman traveled with some money, horses, and his men;
Waited at the prophet's door to be invited in.
Ride horse.

Elisha just sent a message; he would not come to the door.
"Go to the river Jordan. Dip seven times and be restored."
Hold up 7 fingers.

Naaman raged and gnashed his teeth, "This will never do.
He wouldn't even talk to me, and now I feel so blue."
Stomp feet.

His servant said, "My master, the river is nearby.
You do hard things all the time; just give this thing a try."
Make wavy motion for river; shake finger.

One dip, two dips, three dips four,
Five, six, seven dips, and no more.
Dip 7 times.

Naaman left the water and saw that he was cured.
"The God of Israel is true; of that I'm very sure."
Raise arms in praise.

HEALTH
Talk about how God works through doctors and medicine to make us better. Discuss health care: If cut, tell parent or teacher. Wash cuts with soap and water.

Naaman Refrain

2 Kings 5:1–14

Naaman was sick.
  Naaman was sad.
Look sad.

God made him well.
  Then he was glad.
Look happy.

A little girl helped—
  no bigger than you.
Point to children.

She told him of God.
  She said, "He loves you."
Hug self.

We can help others.
  We can tell too.
Cup hands around mouth.

Jesus, who loves us,
  loves others too.
Point to self and others.

~~~~~~

GOD'S PEOPLE IN EXILE

~~~~~~

Three Men in the Fiery Furnace

Daniel 3

The king made a big statue of pure gold.
Reach high.

"Pray to the statue," the people were told,
Fold hands in prayer.

"Or into a fiery furnace you will go."
Point.

But three faithful friends just said, "No."
Shake head no.

"We only pray to God," the three men said.
Fold hands in prayer.

So they were thrown into the furnace,
fiery red.
Make throwing motion.

The king was as surprised as he could be.
Put hands on face, surprised.

He saw four men instead of three!
Hold up 4 fingers.

God had heard the three men pray.
Fold hands in prayer.

And sent His Helper to save them that day.
Cross arms over chest.

ART
Draw a picture of the story.

Daniel in the Lions' Den

Daniel 6

"Pray to me or be thrown to
the lions," said the king.
Fold hands; use fingers to make crown.

But Daniel obeyed God and
wouldn't do such a thing.
Shake head no.

Daniel prayed to God.
Fold hands.

So they threw him to the lions
and slammed the door.
Clap hands once.

But Daniel wasn't afraid
of the hungry lions' roar.
Roar.

Daniel prayed to God.
Fold hands.

God sent an angel to shut
the lions' mouths tight.
Cover mouth.

He kept faithful Daniel safe
all through the night.
Put head on hands.

Daniel prayed to God.
Fold hands.

SPIRITUAL DEVELOPMENT
Talk about things that children are afraid
of and how God is with them and cares for
them.

Esther

The Book of Esther

The king said, "Who will be a wife for me?
Let's have a contest to see who it will be."
Shrug shoulders, palms up.

Women came to the palace to be seen,
And the king chose Esther to be his queen.
Make crown on head with open hand.

One day, Esther heard some bad news.
Haman wanted to kill God's people, the Jews!
Cup ear; look frightened.

So Esther prayed and asked God to help her.
Then she invited Haman and the king to dinner.
Fold hands; then pretend to eat.

The very next day Esther told the king,
"Haman has tricked you into doing a bad thing.
Make crown on head with open hand; shake finger.

The new law will kill all God's people and me."
When the king heard this, he was so angry.
Point to self; point to ears.

Haman was punished for what he had done.
And God's people were saved—every one.
Clap hands.

God used Queen Esther to set the people free.
And He sent His Son, Jesus, to save you and me.
Make sign of the cross, point to others, then self.

EMOTIONAL DEVELOPMENT
Have the children express how they would feel if they were Esther or the king.

~~~~~~~~~~~~~~~~~~~~~~~~~~
THE CHRISTMAS STORY
~~~~~~~~~~~~~~~~~~~~~~~~~~

Birth of John Foretold

Luke 1:5–25

God's priest Zechariah was old and sad.
A boy or girl he wanted, but none he had.
Shake head sadly.

Then the angel Gabriel came to tell,
"God will make you happy! Listen well!
Cup ears.

For your wife, Elizabeth, will have a boy,
Your very own baby; he'll bring much joy!"
Rock baby in arms.

Yes, little baby John soon will come.
He'll grow up to point others to God's Son.
Point; make cross with fingers.

SOCIAL DEVELOPMENT:
The angel told Zechariah and Mary good news. Who tells you good news? What are some of the things you hear?

The Annunciation

Luke 1:26–38

Mary saw an angel.
Shade eyes.

First, she was afraid.
Cover eyes.

Then she listened carefully.
Cup ear.

This is what he said:
Point to mouth.

"You will have a Baby,
Rock baby.

Jesus, God's own Son.
Point up.

He will be the Savior
Make cross with fingers.

Sent for everyone."
Point to others.

ART
Have children draw a picture of an angel. Talk about what they think angels look like and what they do.

Mary Visits Elizabeth

Luke 1:26–56

"Elizabeth, Elizabeth, I'm visiting today.
It's your cousin Mary, and I have a lot to say!
Cup hands around mouth, calling.

I'm going to have a Baby—God's own dear Son.
He will grow and save the world before His work is done.
Rock baby in arms.

The angel also told me that you will have a boy,
My soul rejoices in my God; I've never had such joy!"
Raise palms and eyes to sky.

Then Elizabeth answered Mary, "My unborn baby boy
Just moved when I heard your words. He, too, has jumped for joy!"
Jump.

And so the cousins praised the Lord; their miracles now small,
When grown, would bring light to the world, God's saving love for all.
Hug self.

CRITICAL THINKING
Discuss other ways to tell people news besides
going to see them, such as the phone, Internet,
mail, TV, and radio.

The Birth of John

Luke 1:57–80

Elizabeth had a baby boy.
Rock baby.

He gave his parents such great joy!
Make happy face.

Many friends and neighbors came.
Walk in place.

To see the baby and hear his name.
Rock baby.

"Call him Zechariah," they all said.
Nod head in agreement.

But Zechariah just shook his head.
Shake head no.

"His name is John," he wrote with a pen.
Pretend to write.

And then, Zechariah could speak again!
Put hands on side of face, surprised.

INTELLECTUAL DEVELOPMENT
List the children's names and have them identify their name.
Encourage them to copy their names on paper.

An Angel Visits Joseph

Matthew 1:18–25

Joseph saw an angel
Look up.

While he was sleeping in his bed.
Rest head on hands.

The angel had important news.
Nod yes.

This is what he said:
Touch lips.

"Mary will have a Baby.
Rock baby.

Jesus, God's own Son.
Point up.

He will be the Savior.
Make cross with fingers.

Sent for everyone."
Point to others.

The Birth of Jesus

Luke 2:1–20

Joseph knocked, "May we stay, in your inn for a few days?
My wife, Mary, needs a room. She will have a Baby soon."
Knock on door.

"No rooms here or anywhere, but a cattle stall is there.
You may use it for a bed, a warm place to lay your head."
Lay head on hands.

In Bethlehem before the morn, the tiny Baby soon was born.
In a manger lay the child, Jesus, Savior, meek and mild.
Rock baby.

Shepherds in a field near by saw angels praising God on high,
"Glory be to God above! He has sent the King of Love!
Shade eyes with hand, looking up.

"Find the Savior as a Babe, wrapped and in a manger laid.
Christ is born! Go shout the news! This is God's great sign to you."
Walk in place.

"Here He is!" the shepherds said. "Right here in a manger bed!
We must go tell everyone that this wee Baby is God's Son!"
Cup hands around mouth.

Happy birthday, Baby King!
   Peace, and joy, and love
   You bring.
All who would believe in
   You get this Christmas
   present too.
Put hands on heart.

MUSIC
Learn "Angels We Have Heard on High."

83

Christmas Night

Luke 2:8–18

On the very first Christmas night,
Hold up 1 finger.

Angels filled the dark, dark night.
Twinkle hands above head.

They told the shepherds where Jesus lay,
Cradle baby in arms.

So they could hurry to Him and pray.
Fold hands in prayer.

Baby Jesus

Luke 2:12

Let's gently rock Baby Jesus.
Hold Him in your arms.
Rock baby.

Lay Him in His manger bed.
Keep Him safe and warm.
Put baby in bed.

Tiny little Baby Jesus
Came from heaven above,
Point to heaven.

Came to save us from our sins,
Gives us God's own love.
Hug self.

SOCIAL DEVELOPMENT
Talk about ways to care for babies.

Here Is the Stable

Luke 2:8–16; Matthew 2:1–11

Point to a stable and the nativity figures in it as you say the rhyme.

Here is the stable on Christmas Day.

Here is the manger where Jesus lay.

Here are the angels dressed in white.

Here are the shepherds they told that night.

Here are the Wise Men, following the star.

Here are the camels they rode so far.

Here are the gifts the Wise Men bring.

Here is little Jesus, our Savior
and King.

ART
Have children draw a picture to illustrate part of the poem.

The Presentation of Jesus

Luke 2:22–40

Simeon was old and gray, but still his faith was strong.
"I get to see the Savior, before my time is gone.
> *Make muscle arm; point to eyes.*

I'm trusting in God's promise, the Savior I will see.
That Baby in the temple—please bring Him here to me."
> *Rock baby; motion to come over.*

Then Simeon blessed Jesus, just a few weeks old, so small.
"I am at peace. This child brings salvation for us all."
> *Hold baby; point to self and others.*

A prophetess named Anna said, "Yes, this is the One.
I also thank and praise the Lord for sending down His Son."
> *Nod head.*

His parents thought about their words, so marvelous and true.
And so young Jesus grew in grace, in strength and wisdom too.
> *Squat, grow tall.*

SCIENCE
Explore patterns of growth by illustrating the life cycle of a butterfly. Use a black marker to divide paper plates into four quarters. Glue rice and pastas to the sections in this order: rice, spiral pasta, shell pasta, bow-tie pasta to stand for eggs (rice), caterpillar (spiral pasta), chrysalis/cocoon (shell pasta), and an adult butterfly (bow-tie pasta). Color with markers.

The Visit of the Wise Men

Matthew 2

Jesus was born on Christmas night.
Angels sang "Gloria"—oh, what a sight!
> *Pretend to hold book and sing.*

Up in the sky, God put a big star
That men from the East saw from afar.
> *Point to star.*

They jumped on their camels and rode away.
Bumpity bump, they rode night and day.
> *Bounce up and down.*

Finally, they stopped in Jerusalem,
Thinking King Herod would surely help them.
> *Make crown with hands.*

But when they asked, "Where's the new king?"
Herod just frowned, not knowing a thing.
> *Frown; shrug shoulders.*

Then he called for his teachers, who together all said,
"You'll find Him in Bethlehem; that's what we've read.
> *Make open book with hands.*

Then off rode the Wise Men to Bethlehem town.
They followed God's star, up hill and down.
> *Pretend to ride; point to star.*

Yes, this star in the heavens showed them the way
To the house where little boy Jesus played.
> *Form roof with hands.*

The Wise Men were happy; they were filled with joy!
They got off their camels and worshiped the Boy.
> *Fold hands over heart.*

Kneeling, they gave Him their gifts, for you see,
Jesus is the Savior God sent for you and me.
> *Point to others and then self.*

CRITICAL THINKING
Ask, What do you think the Wise Men saw as they traveled to Bethlehem?

Young Jesus

Matthew 2:19–23

Young Jesus grew
    in Naz'reth,
Was gentle as a dove.
> *Squat, then stand up.*

He *went to school,
    like I do;
He loved as God above.
> *Hug self; point up.*

*Repeat the four-line poem several times. Each time, substitute one of the following phrases and actions for "went to school":

* clapped His hands
* ate His meals
* scraped His knee
* washed His face
* ran outdoors
* slept all night

DRAMATIC PLAY
Have children take turns to pantomime more actions while the others guess what is being acted out.

The Boy Jesus in the Temple

Luke 2:41–52

Jesus was walking with His friends
and family.
Walk in place.

They were going to the temple in
the big city
Point.

To worship God and listen to His
Word.
Open hands like book.

Jesus wanted to remember
everything He heard.
Put hand behind ear.

Finally, it was time to go back
home.
Point in opposite direction.

So they walked and walked the way
they had come.
Walk in place.

When Mary and Joseph stopped for
the night,
Stand still.

They looked for Jesus, but He was
nowhere in sight.
Put hand over eyes, searching.

So they hurried back and ran
through the big city.
Run in place.

They searched high and low, but
their Son they did not see.
Put hand over eyes, searching.

But when they came to the temple
in Jerusalem,
Run in place.

They found Him with the teachers,
talking to them.
Stop and point.

The teachers listened to what Jesus
had to say.
Cup hand behind ear.

His questions and answers amazed
them that day.
Put hands on side of face, surprised.

When we go to God's house, we
hear God's Word too.
Open hands like book.

We hear how much Jesus loves us—
me and you!
Cross arms over heart; point to self and others.

SPIRITUAL DEVELOPMENT
Tell how you worship God in church.

〜〜〜〜〜〜〜〜〜〜〜〜〜〜〜〜
JESUS AND JOHN THE BAPTIST
〜〜〜〜〜〜〜〜〜〜〜〜〜〜〜〜

John Prepares the Way

Matthew 3:1–12; John 1:29–34

John lived by the Jordan River.
Make rippling hand motion.

He wore clothes made of camel hair.
Point to clothes.

John ate locusts and wild honey.
Pretend to eat.

God gave him a message to share.
Point up.

John told the people about God.
Cup hands around mouth.

He baptized them in the river too.
Cup hand; pour water.

He said, "Someone is coming soon.
Hold out hands, palms up.

He's the Savior for me and you."
Hug self.

CRITICAL THINKING
Pretend you are by the river. What are some of the things you might see and hear?

The Baptism of Jesus

Matthew 3:13–17; Luke 3:15–22

Jesus walked down to the river.
Walk.

So John could baptize Him that day.
Cup hand; pour water.

When they came up out of the water,
Walk in place.

The sky opened in an amazing way.
Spread hands apart.

All the people were surprised to see
Put hands on side of face.

God's Spirit come down like a dove.
Lock thumbs, flutter fingers.

Then they heard a voice call from heaven.
Point up.

God said, "This is My Son, whom I love."
Hug self.

SENSES/SPIRITUAL DEVELOPMENT
Allow children to touch and handle things connected to Baptism—the baptismal font, water, napkin, and so forth.

The Temptation of Jesus

Matthew 4:1–11; Luke 4:1–13

Jesus was in the wilderness for forty days.
The devil came and tempted Him in many ways.

Tiptoe in place, arms up and curled, looking sneaky.

Jesus had no food to eat; He was so hungry.
So the devil came and whispered, "Listen to me.

Rub tummy; put hands around mouth and whisper.

If You are *really* God, change these stones into bread!"
But Jesus answered, "No, I won't do what you said."

Shake head no.

Next the sneaky devil took Him way up high
And showed dear Jesus ev'rything under the sky.

Make sweeping motion.

"Worship me," said the devil. "That's all You have to do.
Then all these things will belong to You.

Hold hands out, palms up.

And You will be the ruler over all You see."
But Jesus said, "No, I won't do what you ask of Me."

Shake head no.

But the sneaky old devil wasn't ready to stop.
He then took Jesus to the temple—to the very top!

Reach high.

"If You're *really* the Son of God, jump off," said he.
"You won't get hurt, so don't fret or worry—

Jump; shake head no.

God's angels will protect You; it says so in God's Word."
But Jesus said, "The Bible says, 'Do not test the Lord.'"

Hold hands like book; shake head no.

Then the devil left.

Tiptoe in place, arms up and curled, looking sneaky.

Yes, Jesus said no to the devil; He wouldn't let him win.
He kept God's Law for all of us to save us from our sins.

Shake head no. On "us," point to self and others.

BEHAVIOR MODIFICATION
Have children think of some temptations. Talk about how God helps us say no to temptations.

~~~~~~
JESUS AND THE DISCIPLES
~~~~~~

Jesus Calls the First Disciples

Matthew 4:18–22

Imagine you are fishing and throwing out a net.
You haul the fish into the boat; now you're soaking wet!
Throw net.

The fish with scales a-glitter are flopping everywhere.
Grab and sort them quickly; get that big one over there!
Grab for fish.

But then a voice calls to you, so clear above the din.
The voice says "Follow Me. I'll make you fishers of men."
Beckon with hand.

You look to see who's speaking by the Sea of Galilee.
The voice belongs to Jesus, calling out to you and me.
Point to others, then to self.

And so it was for Simon Peter, Andrew, James, and John.
They left their boats, they left their nets, to follow God the Son.
Walk in place.

They'd cast out nets of love, to people far and near.
They'd tell of Jesus' empty tomb, a gift from God so dear.
Point around; cup hands around mouth.

He's called you, too, to follow Him, as fisher girls and boys.
Now cast your nets for Jesus; let's share His peace and joy!
Beckon to come along.

SCIENCE

All fish live in water and breathe using water. Other animals look like fish but have to come up for air. Sit in a circle with a basket of plastic fish, whales, and dolphins. Sort out the fish after showing how the dolphins and whale models have blowholes for air. Show children how to make the fish symbol and talk about how early Christians used a fish symbol to show they believed in Jesus.

Jesus Calls Philip and Nathanael

John 1:43–51

As Jesus traveled on His way, He came to Galilee.
He found a man named Philip and said, "Philip, follow Me."
Beckon to come along.

Philip told Nathanael, "The promised One is here."
It's Jesus, who's from Nazareth. Come, see, it is so clear!
Jump and clap.

Nathanael rolled his eyes and asked, "Can anything that's good
Come from lowly Nazareth? Not from that place—nothing could!"
Roll eyes; shake head.

Still Nathanael went to see, to look with his own eyes.
Jesus saw him and then said, "This man speaks truth, not lies."
Walk in place.

Nathanael, puzzled, asked Him, "How do You know of me?"
"Before Philip came to you, I saw you neath a tree."
Extend arms above head.

"Jesus, You're the Son of God, the King of Israel!"
"Nathanael, follow Me, and you'll see greater things as well.
Point to eyes and nod.

You'll see God's holy angels as they go to and fro
From heaven to the Son of Man, His glory to behold."
Use hands to make angel wings.

And so Nathanael followed Him, and Philip followed too.
We're also called to follow Him, till all hear the Good News.
Walk in place.

GAME
Play "Mirror." Have children watch closely and copy everything you do no matter how silly. Jesus calls us to follow Him. He gives us His Spirit to help us share His love with others.

Jesus Calls Matthew

Mark 2:13–17

Matthew had a job; some might think it funny.
He was a tax collector, and you *had* to give him money!
Hand over money.

The people did not like this! They didn't want to pay!
The taxes went to Romans, who were mean to them each day.
Stomp foot; say "grrr."

Since Matthew took the taxes, few would be his friends.
People stayed away from him each day when work would end.
Draw tears with fingers.

But Jesus sees with different eyes, and He can make us whole.
He called to Matthew, "Follow Me," for Jesus loves each soul.
Beckon to come along.

Matthew followed Jesus. That night they met for dinner.
The Pharisees began to whisper, "Jesus eats with sinners!"
Walk in place. Whisper, "Jesus eats with sinners!"

But Jesus stopped to teach them, "The good do not need Me.
I've come to call those sick in sin and heal them, don't you see?"
Shake head no; hug self.

Since everyone is sick with sin, and none are good or pure,
We thank You, Jesus, for the cross, and that You are sin's cure!
Make cross with fingers; say, "Thank You, Jesus!"

HEALTH

Sickness is in the world because of sin, but God has given us doctors to help us. Teach proper hand washing and how to cough or sneeze into the inner elbow, not hands. Talk about how helping to not spread germs shows love to others.

Matthew

Matthew 5:27–28

Matthew was a greedy man, as greedy as could be.
Make a grumpy face.

Till Jesus said, "Hey, Matthew! Leave those taxes; follow Me."
Beckon with hand.

Then Matthew started smiling with the biggest smile he had.
Smile broadly.

And went around with Jesus, making other people glad.
Walk in place.

92

Jesus Changes Water into Wine

John 2:1–11

Put your best clothes on, and we will have some fun.
We're going to a wedding. The party's just begun.
Pretend to dress.

We'll travel now to Cana, and at this great affair,
Jesus, plus His mother and disciples, will be there.
Look around and point.

Oh, look, there is a problem! The wine is running out!
The couple will feel bad if their guests must do without!
Hold hands, palms up, look worried.

Mary, Jesus' mother, says, "Jesus, there's no wine!"
Jesus says, "Why come to Me? You know it's not My time."
Use questioning look; point to self.

His mother tells the servers, "Do anything He asks."
They fill six jars with water, as He directs their tasks.
Fill jars with water.

A miracle takes place! The water turns to wine!
A helper tells the groom, "This last wine is quite fine!"
Jump and clap.

Jesus showed His power while at this wedding dinner,
And by His power on the cross, saints are made from
    sinners.
Make sign of the cross.

MUSIC
Jesus did miracles to help others, such as this bride and groom, and fulfill what the Old Testament said God's Messiah would do. We can help others as a way to share His love. Sing "Jesus Wants Me for a Helper."

Jesus Teaches Nicodemus

John 3:1–21

Nicodemus worshiped God. He was a Pharisee.
Some questions buzzed inside his head, just like a bumblebee.
Tap head.

He waited until nighttime. To Jesus, he would go.
He'd finally get some answers; he knew the Lord would know.
Walk in place.

"To enter into heaven, you must be free of sin."
Jesus said, "I tell the truth; you must be born again."
Point to heaven.

"How can that be the answer?" the Pharisee declared.
"I can't become a baby. I'm old and have gray hair!"
Stroke beard.

"What God the Holy Spirit does cannot be done by man.
You're born again with water, Word; it is God's saving plan.
Pretend to baptize.

Don't you know God loves mankind in spite of sin and strife?
He sent His Son so those in faith have everlasting life."
Cross hands over heart.

So celebrate your Baptism, when you were born again.
By water and the Word, Jesus washed away your sin!
Rub one hand on the other to wash.

SCIENCE

Water is needed for life on earth. Use celery stalks with leaves. Put some in glasses of water, others in dry glasses. Observe over a few days and describe the differences. Add water to the dry glasses and observe the differences. In Baptism, the Spirit works through God's Word and water to forgive our sins for Jesus' sake and make us God's children. He comes to live in us and give us new life.

Jesus and the Samaritan Woman

John 4:1–42

There were two groups of people, Samaritans and Jews.
They didn't like each other; their feelings had been bruised.
Pound fist into other hand.

A woman from Samaria, as this story will tell,
Spoke to Jesus when He asked for water from a well.
Pretend to take a drink.

"It's odd that You should speak to me," the woman did reply.
"Your people will not deal with us. They shoo us like we're flies."
Shoo flies with hands.

Jesus said, "God sent a gift, and if you only knew,
You'd ask Me for the *living* water I can give to you.
Use hands to make ripples.

Whoever drinks well water will always thirst again,
Who drinks God's living water gains life in heaven with Him.
Point to heaven.

For only living water revives the sin-parched soul."
He told the woman of her sins and how God makes us whole.
Use hands to make ripples. Wilt, then stand tall.

She ran to tell the others, "Come with me, and you'll see.
This man could be the Christ; He knew secrets about me!"
Run in place.

So whether you are girls or boys, Samaritans or Jews,
Jesus loves you all the same; His water is for you too.
Open arms wide.

ART

God sent Jesus for everyone. Use magazines, coloring pages, or computer printouts. Cut out pictures of people all ages, sizes, and races. Glue or staple them into a giant circle collage on a bulletin board. Put a construction-paper cross in the center.

~~~~~~~~~~~~~~~~~~~~~~~~~~~~~~~~~~~~

JESUS DOES MANY MIRACLES

~~~~~~~~~~~~~~~~~~~~~~~~~~~~~~~~~~~~

Jesus Rejected at Nazareth

Luke 4:16–30

Jesus started teaching where the Jews would come to learn.
In the synagogue, men read God's Word, and Jesus took a turn.
> *Pretend to read.*

"I'm reading from Isaiah, God's truth for great and small.
God says the blind will one day see; the Savior will free all.
> *Cover eyes; then remove hands.*

This Scripture has come true today, as you surely heard."
At first, the Jewish men praised Jesus for His gracious words.
> *Smile and nod.*

But then He said the Lord would offer His salvation,
Not to the chosen Jews alone, but to all faithful nations.
> *Open arms wide.*

This news angered the Jews so much, they forced Him out of town.
But Jesus calmly walked away, and He was never harmed.
> *Walk in place.*

Jesus kept on teaching all; He made God's Word more clear.
He wanted everyone to know He was their Savior dear.
> *Make cross with fingers; hug self.*

MUSIC
God's Word is written in many languages so all may come to Christ. Teach chorus of "Amigos de Cristo."

Jesus Heals Many

Luke 4:31–44

Jesus walked down to the town—Capernaum by name.
That Sabbath Day He taught God's Word and helped a man who came.
> *Walk; reach out hands.*

An evil spirit in that man had made his life no fun.
That spirit spoke to Jesus saying, "You're the Holy One."
> *Point.*

Then to the evil spirit, Jesus said, "Come out of him."
The evil one came out—Hooray! The man was well again.
> *Clap.*

Peter had a mother-in-law, sick with a fever hot.
When Jesus called that fever out, she got up from her cot.
> *Put hand on forehead; jump up.*

Yes, Jesus healed so many with
    His word and gentle touch.
But His best cure is for our sin;
    for this, we love Him much.
> *Cross hands over heart.*

So when you get a boo-boo or
    are sick in bed all day,
You, too, can pray to Jesus, who
    will hear all that you say.
> *Fold hands.*

HEALTH
Thorough hand washing helps people stay healthy.
Pretend to rub hands with soap as you sing the
"Alphabet Song" (the recommended twenty-five
seconds). Then pretend to rinse them.

Jesus Heals a Paralyzed Man

Mark 2:1–12

When Jesus came to Capernaum, the news spread far and wide.
From left and right the people came; the room was full inside.
> *Point left, then right.*

A man who couldn't move at all was brought there by some friends.
They hoped that Jesus, with a touch, would help him move again.
> *Stand with stiff body.*

"The door is blocked!" the four men said. "Let's climb up to the top.
We'll make a hole in the roof." Those four men never stopped!
> *Walk up steps and make a hole in roof.*

With ropes they gently lowered down the paralytic man.
Soon Jesus saw the men, their faith, and shared His healing plan.
> *Move arms as if lowering ropes.*

And all nearby heard Jesus say, "Your sins are washed away."
He also said, "Rise, take your bed, and now walk on your way."
> *Lift hands; walk in place.*

Quickly, the man picked up his bed and walked before the crowd.
The people cheered and praised the Lord with words amazed aloud.
> *Walk in place; clap.*

Yes, Jesus is God's Son who heals; His power can make us well.
But best of all, He gives the cure for sin and death and hell.
> *Make cross with fingers.*

SOCIAL DEVELOPMENT
Talk about how to show respect and care for people with disabilities.

Jesus Calms a Storm

Mark 4:35–41

Jesus and His followers were riding in a boat.
Jesus even took a nap, so gentle was the float.
Put head on hands.

But suddenly a windstorm whipped up the waves so high.
Water came into the boat; it looked like they might die.
Make wind sounds.

"Get up and save us, Jesus! This boat is going down!
Don't You care about our lives? We think we're going to drown!"
Clasp hands, pleading.

"Where's your faith?" He scolded them. "Be still," He told the sea.
The waves obeyed, the wind died down, as peaceful as could be.
Shake finger, show calm with hands out flat.

When everything was calm, the disciples were amazed.
But Jesus wanted them to trust, *not* to be afraid.
Put hands on sides of face; cross arms over chest.

So when the winds are blowing, and you are shaking too,
Call on Jesus, ask for help, He knows just what to do.
Fold hands in prayer.

SAFETY
Talk about water safety. Tell children not to use floating objects to go on the water by themselves or walk on a frozen pond unless they are with a parent.

Jesus Heals Jairus's Daughter

Mark 5:21–24, 35–43

Jairus had a daughter who was twelve but sick in bed.
If someone could not help her, he was sure she would be dead.
  Close eyes.

So Jairus came to Jesus, bowed, and begged, "Please come with me!
"O Jesus, touch her with Your hand and heal her thoroughly!"
  Kneel, begging.

They walked and met some people with a message to relay,
"There is no need to bring this man; your daughter's passed away."
  Shake head sadly.

Then Jesus spoke to Jairus, saying, "Fear not; just believe."
He made His way into the house and talked to those who grieved.
  Pat shoulder.

He stood beside the little child and gently took her hand.
"Arise, I say, O little girl." She woke and rose to stand!
  Crouch down low; then stand up.

This loving Jesus is with us; He gives us life and breath.
We praise His name and celebrate; He's even beaten death.
  Clap; make cross with fingers.

SERVICE
Put cross or Christian stickers on bandages; put the bandages in ziplock bags to give to shut-ins.

Jesus Walks on Water

Matthew 14:22–33

Jesus made His helpers get into a boat one day.
But He went on a mountain to find a place to pray.
Fold hands to pray.

In the night, a wind so strong began to blow and blow.
In the boat, the strong winds made it very hard to go.
Blow; sway side to side.

In the night walked Jesus to the men across the sea.
He stayed on top of water; oh, my, who could it be?
Walk in place.

The men, now terrified, thought a ghost was walking by!
But Jesus said, "Take heart. Don't be afraid. It is I."
Look scared; hold hands out; point to self.

Peter wondered. Peter said, "Call me to walk to You."
So Peter crawled out bravely when Jesus told him to.
Crawl out of boat.

Whoosh! Peter saw the wind making waves upon the sea.
Yikes! Peter sank and cried out, "O Lord, please save me!"
Make big waves with hands; sink down.

Then Jesus stretched out His hand to Peter sinking low.
In the boat, the two men stepped; the wind then ceased to blow.
Stretch out hand; step.

When you feel a whoosh of fear and you are sinking too,
Look to Jesus and have faith. He died and rose for you.
Hands over heart; make cross with fingers.

SCIENCE
Talk about storms and some of the things that can be heard, seen, and felt in a storm.

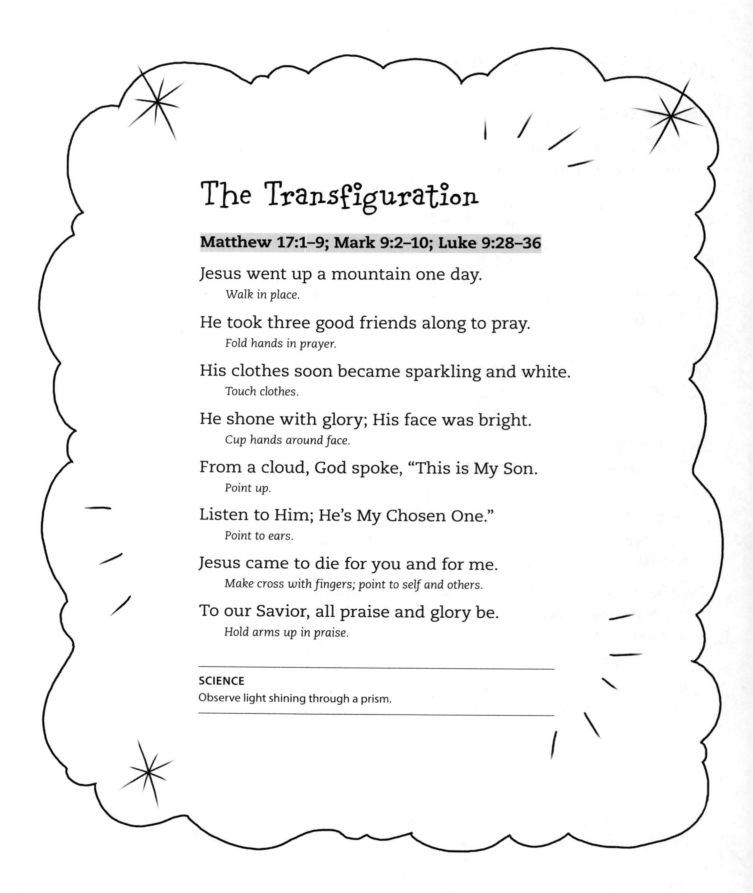

The Transfiguration

Matthew 17:1–9; Mark 9:2–10; Luke 9:28–36

Jesus went up a mountain one day.
Walk in place.

He took three good friends along to pray.
Fold hands in prayer.

His clothes soon became sparkling and white.
Touch clothes.

He shone with glory; His face was bright.
Cup hands around face.

From a cloud, God spoke, "This is My Son.
Point up.

Listen to Him; He's My Chosen One."
Point to ears.

Jesus came to die for you and for me.
Make cross with fingers; point to self and others.

To our Savior, all praise and glory be.
Hold arms up in praise.

SCIENCE
Observe light shining through a prism.

Jesus Heals a Blind Man

John 9

A blind man sat by the temple begging.
One day, Jesus and His friends came walking by.

> *Hold hand out, palm up; walk.*

Jesus came over to the man and spit on the ground.
He made mud of the spit and put it on the man's eyes.

> *Pick up mud and put it on eyes.*

Then Jesus said, "Wash off the mud in the pool."
So the man washed his eyes as he was told to do.

> *Wash eyes.*

When Jesus opened the blind man's eyes, the blind man could see.
He saw the people around him, and he saw Jesus too.

> *Look and point all around.*

With his mouth he said to Jesus, "Lord, I do believe."
Jesus helped the blind man see, and Jesus helps us too.

> *Touch mouth; touch eyes.*

He helps us see that He is God with special eyes of faith.
He helps us to tell others, "Jesus makes all things new."

> *Touch eyes; cup hands around mouth; make cross with fingers.*

COLOR IDENTIFICATION
The blind man couldn't see any colors. What colors do you see in the room?

~~~~~~~~~~~~~~~~~~~~~~~~~~~~~~~~

JESUS TEACHES AND PREACHES

~~~~~~~~~~~~~~~~~~~~~~~~~~~~~~~~

The Beatitudes

Matthew 5:1–12

One day on a mountain, Jesus sat down and taught people how they are blessed.

Sit; open hands like book.

He said, "Blessed are the unhappy who sin—God makes them feel better."

Look sad; hug self.

He said, "Blessed are the humble—God will give them great things."

Bow head; raise head and lift hands.

He said, "Blessed are the merciful—God sees their troubles and helps."

Stretch out hands, palms up.

He said, "Blessed are the peacemakers—God calls them His children."

Hug self.

INTELLECTUAL DEVELOPMENT
Define the word *blessed*. Have children tell of God's blessings to them.

Jesus Clears the Temple

John 2:13–22

Jesus went into the temple to pray
And found people buying and selling that day.

Fold hands; look around.

Birds, sheep, and goats were all moving about.
But this trading was bad; He chased sellers out.

Walk in place; shake finger.

Tables fell over; coins spilled on the floor.
He said, "Don't sell things in this place anymore.

Twinkle fingers; shake head no.

This is God's house; people come here each day.
They come here to worship; they come here to pray."

Point up; fold hands in prayer.

SPIRITUAL DEVELOPMENT
Have children tell how they
worship God in church.

Jesus Tells about God's Care

Matthew 6:25–34

God feeds the birds up in the air.
They don't worry or have a care.

Flap arms like wings; shake head.

God gives sun above and rain below.
So flowers don't worry how they will grow.

Make sun and rain motions. Crouch and grow tall.

Since God cares for the birds and flowers,
Have faith He'll care for you each hour.

Flap arms; smell flowers; point to others.

He gives us everything we need.
He is our loving God indeed.

Open arms wide; cross hands over chest.

INTELLECTUAL DEVELOPMENT
Name ways that you can care for birds and plants.

Jesus Feeds Five Thousand

Matthew 15:29–38

Luke 12:22–34

John 6:1–14

Row, row across the lake.
Climb, climb up the hill.

Row; climb.

Teach, teach until too late.
Hungry, hungry folks to fill.

Hold hands like book; rub stomach.

Share, share a boy's lunch.
Pray, pray with thanks to God.

Offer gift; fold hands.

Break, break fish and bread.
Eat, eat—now all are fed.

Break bread; eat.

Gather, gather up the scraps.
Thank You, thank You, Jesus!

Gather; fold hands.

Blessings, blessings every day.
Thank You, thank You, Jesus!

Hold hands open; raise both arms.

SPIRITUAL DEVELOPMENT
Talk about how God cares for us. Invite children to share table prayers.

JESUS TEACHES AND PREACHES

Jesus Is Anointed

Luke 7:36–50

"Jesus, come," said Simon, "we'll have some food to eat.
A woman heard Jesus was there and sat down near His feet.
Eat, walk in place, and then sit.

Her loving tears made His feet wet. Her perfume filled the air.
The woman poured it on His feet; then dried them with her hair.
Draw tears on face with fingers; touch hair.

Simon said, "This woman's done bad things. Tell her she must go."
But Jesus said, "Her sins are forgiven because I love her so."
Wag finger; hug self.

Jesus knows we've done bad things, the things that we call sin.
But He has died to pay for sin, and then He rose again.
Wag finger; make cross with fingers.

EMOTIONAL DEVELOPMENT
How do you think the woman felt when Jesus said He loved her? How can you show your love to Jesus?

Jesus Sends Out Seventy-two

Luke 10:1–24

Jesus gave these directions to seventy-two helpers. He sent them ahead of Him to places He would go.

You will travel two by two,
Speaking to believers true.

Show 2 sets of 2 fingers.

Pray to God to send us more
Helpers for this heav'nly chore.

Pray; then march.

Travel light without a bag,
Sack, or extra stuff to drag.

Walk in place.

In a city that is new,
Stay with those who welcome you.

Open arms in welcome.

If they give you food to eat,
Bless their families with My peace.

Eat and smile.

Say, "God's kingdom has come near,"
Heal the sick, and calm their fear.

Pat head.

If they do not welcome you,
Kick the dust right off your shoes.

Kick dust off shoes.

You'll be like lambs in the wild,
Where some like wolves are mean
    and vile.

Snarl and growl.

All folks that push away My Word
Will wish someday that they had
    heard.

Push with hands; point to ears.

But you rejoice when things aren't
    nice.
For your name is in My Book of Life.

Point to others; open hands like book.

MATH
Write the numeral 72 on the board. Together, count to 72 while putting beans in a jar.

The Good Samaritan

Luke 10:25–37

Jesus told this story to a lawyer who wanted to know what to do to have eternal life. The lawyer knew he should love God and his neighbor, but Jesus helped him see what those words really meant.

"A man once went to Jericho," this is what Jesus said.
"Robbers beat him, took his stuff, and left him there for dead.
    Bend down or fall to ground.

A priest came by and saw him; a Levite also came.
The priest walked by and didn't help; the Levite did the same!
    Walk in place.

And then came a Samaritan; you'd think he'd walk by too.
After all, his people were the enemies of Jews.
    Turn head and cover eyes.

But he was moved by mercy and bandaged that man's skin,
Put him on his animal, and took him to an inn.
    Touch arm; pretend to ride up and down on horse.

Three men saw that hurt man. Who loved him like a friend?
It was the one with mercy, who helped him in the end.
    Show 3 fingers, then 1.

When God says "Love your neighbor," He
    means not just your friends.
God's mercy is for everyone, till
    Jesus comes again.
    Hug self; open arms.

BEHAVIORS
Talk about ways we help each other, such as sharing and not teasing. Practice saying, "I'm sorry," and "Please forgive me."

Jesus, the Good Shepherd

John 10:1–18, 22–30; Psalm 23

Think of Jesus as a shepherd, you His special lamb.
Pretend you're in His flock of sheep, to help you understand.
Say baa.

The Shepherd will protect you, no matter what the cost.
He'll gladly give His life for lambs, so not one lamb is lost.
Make cross with fingers.

The Shepherd knows His lambs by name, and they can trust His call.
He leads them safely through each day, because He loves them all.
Cross arms over heart.

If other shepherds sneak in and lead the lambs astray,
The lambs baa, "You're not my Shepherd!" Then they run away.
Run in place.

When day is done and lambs are led to rest in the sheep pen,
This Shepherd is the only One the gatekeeper lets in.
Make a welcoming gesture.

So little lambs, now hear His voice,
     for He is life and love.
The Good Shepherd is Jesus,
     The way to heav'n above.
Point to sky.

SOCIAL DEVELOPMENT
Talk about how to treat pets. They need clean water and
daily food, brushing, clean cages, and exercise. Don't tease
them or grab their fur. Hold them gently.

Jesus Teaches Us to Pray

Luke 11:1–13; John 16:23–33

The disciples asked,
"Jesus, teach us how to pray.
Tell us what to do and say."
Fold hands.

He said,
"Talk to God, your Father,
He is a loving listener.
Point to mouth.

Hallow His name above.
To do so shows your love.
Point up; cross hands over heart.

Pray His kingdom comes soon.
Help any way you can.
Fold hands; then open them, palms up.

"Pray His good will is done
On earth and heav'n above.
Fold hands; point to sky, then to ground.

Ask Him for food and more;
He gives you gifts galore.
Pretend to eat; open hands to receive.

Ask for forgiveness too.
Forgive those mean to you.
Make cross with fingers.

When you are tempted, pray.
God's help is on the way."
Fold hands.

So, talk to God each day.
He loves it when you pray!
Point to mouth; fold hands and smile.

SPIRITUAL DEVELOPMENT
Pray the Lord's Prayer. Add actions.

Jesus Raises Lazarus

John 11:1–45

A certain man named Lazarus was ill for several days.
Unless someone could heal him, he soon would pass away.
Close eyes.

His sisters sent for Jesus: "Please heal him with Your touch.
Lazarus is dying; our brother suffers much."
Clasp hands, begging.

Jesus did not hurry or rush to Lazarus's side.
He found the sisters at the grave, for Lazarus had died.
Walk in place, slowly.

"O Lord, if You had been here, our brother would have lived.
We know You are the Son of God, and life is Yours to give."
Draw tears on face.

Jesus, too, loved Lazarus and also shed a tear.
"I'll wake him like he's sleeping; with Me death holds no fear.
Pat shoulder.

For I'm the resurrection for all those who believe;
Even though they die, they'll live eternally.
Point to sky.

So Father, now I ask You, from death set Lazarus free.
O Lazarus, come from your grave. Walk over here to Me."
Fold hands in prayer.

Lazarus came walking out, as if he'd never died.
"Only the true Son of God could do this," people cried.
Walk in place; put hands on side of face, surprised.

I love to hear this story. It brings such joy to me!
I know that I will live in heaven, for I, too, do believe.
Place hands on heart.

SCIENCE
Spring reminds us of new life in Jesus. Plant bean seeds in plastic cups filled with potting soil. After some growth, dump out plant on newspaper and describe.

~~~~~~~~~~~~~~~~~~~~~~~~~~~~~~~~~~~~~~~
JESUS GOES TO THE CROSS
~~~~~~~~~~~~~~~~~~~~~~~~~~~~~~~~~~~~~~~

The Prodigal Son

Luke 15:11–32

Once Jesus told this story so people would know about God's forgiving love.

A father had two sons. He loved them both the same.
The younger one was selfish. He wanted cash and fame.
  Show 2 fingers; thumbs-up, boasting.

He said, "I want what's mine, so I can live so grand.
I want to leave and go away, off to a distant land."
  Point to self on "mine"; walk in place.

He spent all he had on parties small and big.
And so he had nothing to eat and went to feed the pigs.
  Rub tummy.

So back to his dad he went, so sorry and so sad.
And he was very sure his father would be mad!
  Run in place; hang head.

But his father was so happy and went to great cost.
To have a big, big party for the son no longer lost.
  Clap hands.

God loves us like this father, and He forgives our sin
Through Jesus Christ, who died for us and three days
  later rose again.
  Hug self; make cross with fingers.

MATH
Draw your family. Chart what
different family members might
need if they went on a trip.

Jesus Heals Ten Men with Leprosy

Luke 17:11–19

Jesus went walking, went walking one day.
He spotted ten men as He went on His way.
> *Walk in place; hold up 10 fingers.*

They cried out, "Have mercy! We're sick and unclean."
They huddled together, chose not to be seen.
> *Huddle with hands over head.*

But Jesus had mercy; then sent them away.
They went off to the priests; there was no delay.
> *Point away; walk in place.*

As they hurried, they noticed that they had been healed.
One quickly returned, and near Jesus, he kneeled.
> *Run in place; show 1 finger.*

He was praising and thanking, not wasting time.
But Jesus wondered aloud, Where were the nine?
> *Hold up arms in praise; show 9 fingers.*

To the one, Jesus said faith had healed him that day.
He was clean, he was saved; then he went on His way.
> *Show 1 finger; make a washing motion over heart; walk in place.*

SOCIAL/SPIRITUAL DEVELOPMENT
Wash the baby dolls in the water table. Make a prayer list.

Jesus Heals Ten Sick Men

Luke 17:11–19

Use fingers to show numerals.

One sick, two sick, three sick men.
Four sick, five sick, six sick men.
Seven sick, eight sick, nine sick men.
Ten men prayed to Jesus.

One sick, two sick, three sick men.
Four sick, five sick, six sick men.
Seven sick, eight sick, nine sick men.
Jesus made them better.

One man, two men, three were healed.
Four men, five men, six were healed.
Seven men, eight men, nine were healed.
But . . .

Use finger to show 1.

Only one came back to say,
"Thank You, Thank You, Jesus!"

Clap on "Thank You, Jesus!"

___

MATH
Set out manipulatives for children to count and sort into groups
of ten.
___

Jesus and the Little Children

Mark 10:13–16

Sing this to the melody of "Jesus Loves the Little Children."

Parents brought their little children to the Savior to be blessed.
When the little ones arrived, oh, they had a big surprise.
"Go away!" They heard the twelve disciples say.
> *Walk forward; stop.*

But when Jesus saw them fussing, He said, "Let the children come.
Do not hinder them this day, for to such as these I say
That the kingdom that I bring belongs to them."
> *Motion to come.*

Jesus took the little children—blessed them as He held them close.
And His Word and deeds are true, for this Jesus loves you too.
And the kingdom that He brings belongs to you.
> *Hug self.*

GAME

Play red light, green light. Cut shapes to make Stop and Go signs. Use red for Stop and green for Go. Put a sad face on the Stop sign and a happy face on the Go sign.

Jesus and Zacchaeus

Luke 19:1–10

When Jesus entered Jericho, Zacchaeus could not see.
When the people blocked his view, this short man climbed up a tree.
Use hand to shade eyes; climb hand over hand.

From high up on the limb, he had a better view.
Then Jesus stopped, looked up at him, and spoke some happy news.
Shade eyes; show surprise.

"Hurry down, Zacchaeus. I want to visit you."
Then Jesus brought salvation to sinful Zacchaeus too.
Climb down hand over hand; make cross with fingers.

Jesus wants to visit us no matter what we've done.
He came to seek and save the lost; for us, salvation won.
Cross hands over heart.

MATH
Make spyglasses out of empty paper-towel rolls. Decorate and spy big and small things around the room.

Gather things in the classroom to arrange by size, smallest to tallest.

The Widow's Mite

Mark 12:41–44

The man with plenty gave some coins.
The man with much gave a few.
> *Drop coins into container.*

The widow gave two little coins.
Her few were more; it's true.
> *Show 2 fingers; nod head.*

The man with plenty gave a part.
The widow gave with all her heart.
> *Hold hands to indicate small amount; cross hands over heart.*

Our gifts come from God's mighty throne.
All that we have is His alone.
> *Open hands; look up.*

ART/MATH
Make coin boxes out of milk containers or some other box and decorate them. Save for a special offering or gift. Count and compare coins.

Jesus Gives the Lord's Supper

Luke 22:1–23

The night He was betrayed, Jesus went to eat
A special meal with His twelve friends, with wine and bread and meat.
  Eat.

He took the bread and broke it, thanked God, and then did say,
"Eat this bread; it is My body, giv'n for you today."
  Break bread and hold it out.

He took the wine and drank it, and then went on to say,
"Drink this wine; it is My blood, giv'n for you this day.
  Drink.

Because My body and My blood are given up for you,
Your sins are washed away, and life will come anew.
  Wash.

But I know someone here has turned his back on Me.
He has betrayed My trust and helped My enemies."
  Frown; shake head.

Judas was the one, the friend who'd taken pay
To tell the priests where Jesus was, so they could have their way.
  Count money in hand.

When you are bigger and
    confirmed, you'll take the
    wine and bread,
The body and the blood of
    Christ, just the way He said.
  Kneel and pray.

MATH
Using pennies, count to thirty. Show how many
pieces of silver Judas received.

Peter Denies Jesus

Mark 14:26–72

Peter spoke to Jesus the night He was betrayed.
He was sad when Jesus said, "In fear, you'll run away."
Make sad face and point to it.

"I'll never leave You, Jesus! I'm sticking to the end.
Even if the others run and You lose all Your friends!"
Pound fist in other palm.

But Jesus warned him clearly—the night would bring a test.
"When the rooster crows, you'll deny Me like the rest."
Crow twice.

Before the rooster crowed two times, Peter had been tested.
"I don't know Him!" he said three times after Jesus was arrested.
Shake head no.

Then Peter broke down, crying, "I gave in to my fear!"
But soon Jesus' forgiveness would wipe away his tears.
Wipe tears away.

SCIENCE

Chickens are birds. They have feathers and lay eggs. Boy
chickens are called roosters. Girl chickens are called hens.
Examine feathers with hand lens. Mimic crowing.

Jesus Dies and Lives Again

Luke 23:26–24:12

The people turned on Jesus: "We want Him dead and gone!"
But first, they had to prove that He'd done something wrong.
Frown; raise arm in air, making a fist.

The ruler Pontius Pilate saw evil in their plan.
He said, "I find no wrong in Him, and we should free this man."
Shake head no as you hold hands open, palms up.

But when he let the crowds choose, they set another free.
"Crucify!" they yelled and screamed. "Nail Jesus to the tree."
Pretend to hammer a nail.

So Jesus, with a crown of thorns, was nailed upon the cross.
As He died between two thieves, His friends thought all was lost.
Draw tears on face.

They put His body in a tomb, a grave cut out of stone.
A rock was placed so everyone would leave the grave alone.
Roll stone.

On Sunday, women went there with spices they had brought.
The rock was moved! Jesus was gone! But angels said, "Fear not!
Look surprised, placing hands on side of face.

For Jesus Christ is living; it is just as He said.
Go tell the others the Good News, 'He's risen from the dead!'"
Clap.

The men did not believe it till Peter ran to see.
"I've seen the tomb with my own eyes. It's empty! I believe!"
Run in place; point to eyes.

We, too, can read the story; we, too, can feel the joy.
This Jesus who was dead now lives—tell every girl and boy!
Point to mouth, then to boys and girls.

MUSIC
Sing "I Have the Joy." Pass rhythm instruments around the circle to play for each stanza.

JESUS RISES FROM THE GRAVE

Easter Morning

Matthew 28:1–8

Long ago when Jesus died,
His friends were very sad.
They missed Him, oh, so much,
   you know.
The world seemed cold and bad.
   Hug self as if shivering; look sad.

On Easter morning, off they went
To visit Jesus' grave.
Slowly, very slowly walked
The women to the cave.
   Walk in place.

When they came close,
   then they could see
The big rock now was gone.
The friends of Jesus peeked inside.
An angel sat alone.
   Put hand over eyes to look.

"He is not here," the angel said.
"For Jesus Christ is risen!"
The friends were very happy now
And told everyone who'd listen.
   Cup hands around mouth.

The day that seemed so dark and sad
Now shone with glory bright.
Jesus' love made all things new.
It was a happy sight.
   Point to corners of mouth in smile.

Jesus makes our days so bright.
His love shines round us too.
Thank You, Jesus, for Your great love
And for the things You do. Amen.
   Clap.

FIVE SENSES

Have children describe Easter morning using as many of their senses as they can. For example, what sounds might they hear? What might they touch or smell? What would they see?

The Empty Tomb

John 20:1–10

Mary Magdalene walked early to the tomb
On a Sunday morning, still dark and filled with gloom.
Walk in place.

The stone was rolled away! The Savior's body gone!
She thought, They've taken Him! I'll tell Peter and John.
Look surprised, hands on side of face.

John and Peter raced. John ran on ahead,
Peeked inside, and saw the cloth that gently wrapped the dead.
Run in place.

Peter walked inside. Could this really be?
Linen cloths, a facecloth too, was all that he could see.
Look around.

The disciples would remember the words that Jesus said.
How He'd die in place of all and rise up from the dead.
Point to head; make cross with fingers; raise arms, palms up.

SPIRITUAL DEVELOPMENT
Open an empty Easter egg. Tell how the empty grave was an Easter gift. It shows how Jesus' resurrection beats death.

Jesus Appears to Mary Magdalene

John 20:11–18

Mary Magdalene had tears streaming down her sad, sad face.
By the tomb she wondered who moved Jesus from this place.
Draw tears on face with fingers.

She stooped and went inside; two angels she did meet.
"Woman, tell us why you're sad. Why is it that you weep?"
Stoop and stand up.

"I'm looking for the body of my Lord and friend.
Someone must have moved it; tell me where if you can."
Hold hands out as though asking for something.

She thought she saw a gardener. "Perhaps he'll tell me more."
But when He said her name, she saw that it was the Lord!
Put hands on sides of face, surprised.

She clung to Him with joy. "Let go," He said with love.
For I have not yet risen to My Father up above."
Point up.

Mary told the others what she'd seen and heard,
Jesus rose up from the dead! Let's all go spread the Word!
Open arms wide.

SERVICE PROJECT
Use stickers and markers to
make Easter cards for shut-ins.

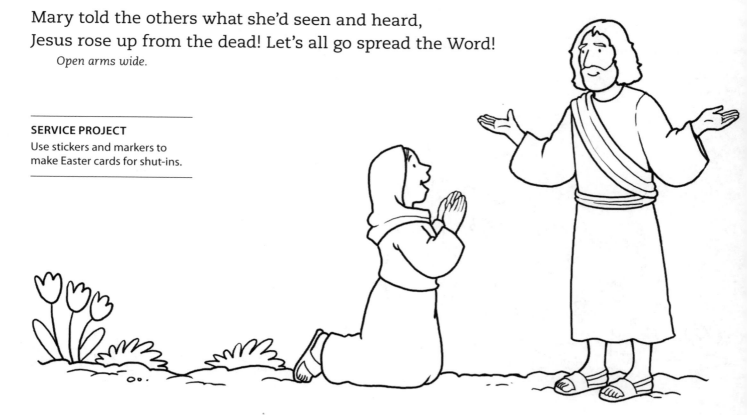

Jesus Appears on the Emmaus Road

Luke 24:13–35

Two sad friends journeyed down a dusty road.
They walked and talked about what they didn't know.
Walk in place.

Up came Jesus and walked along with them.
"What are you saying?" He asked the two friends.
Put hands out as if asking.

He kept them both from seeing who He really was,
As one of them explained why the town was all abuzz.
Point to mouth.

He told the story of the cross, the empty grave they'd seen,
Of prophecies and teachings, of what it all could mean.
Make cross with fingers; open hands, palms up.

Jesus said, "O foolish ones, the prophets told the story
That Christ would suffer, die, and rise, and He'd reign in glory."
Wag finger back and forth; point down, then up.

At dinner, Jesus blessed the bread and then with open eyes,
The two men knew that man was Jesus! Oh, what a surprise!
Put hands on sides of face, surprised.

Yes, Jesus was alive! But He disappeared from view.
With happy hearts the two ran back to tell the joyous news.
Run in place.

MISSIONS
Explain what a missionary is. Go to lcms.org. Find the name of a missionary family and pray for them.

Jesus Appears to Thomas

John 20:19–31

Thomas was a happy man, a joyful man and blest.
He was Jesus' dear disciple friend, just like all the rest.
>   *Hug self.*

When Jesus died and rose again, Thomas said, "Oh, no.
I don't believe; just go away, and leave me to my woe."
>   *Draw tears on face.*

Then Jesus spoke to Thomas; His love was tall and wide.
"Thomas, it is I, you see. Look at My hands and side."
>   *Hold out hands.*

"My Lord and God!" Then Thomas said, "You give me faith again.
Now I believe. Oh, thank You, Lord; I have the joy of ten."
>   *Kneel with hands over heart, smiling; jump up.*

"Oh, blest are those who do not see," said Jesus to them all,
"And yet believe in Me today. I will not let them fall."
>   *Put hands over heart.*

LANGUAGE DEVELOPMENT

Give children turns holding a puppet. Read a statement that can be true or false (e.g., grass is green; the sky is blue; chickens moo; pigs have wings) and ask the child with the puppet, "Do you believe?" Children can move the puppet's head yes or no and say "I do" or "I don't"; then give the puppet to the next child. At the end, talk about what *believe* means and how we can believe what God's Word says about Jesus.

Jesus Reinstates Peter

John 21:1–19

Jesus and Peter ate fish by the sea.
Then Jesus asked Peter, "Do you love Me?"

Use hands to make fish motion; hold up 1 finger with questioning look.

"Yes, Lord," he answered, "You know that I do."
"Feed My lambs," Jesus said, but He wasn't through.

Nod head yes; open hands, palms up, to indicate lambs in front of you.

Again, Jesus asked him, "Do you love Me?"
"Yes, Lord," said Peter that day by the sea.

Hold up 2 fingers.

"Feed My sheep," Jesus answered. Then what did He say?
Once more He asked Peter that question that day.

Hold up 3 fingers.

"I love You," said Peter again and again.
"Feed My sheep, Peter. Tell them I rose from the dead."

Make cross with fingers; raise hands, palms up.

MUSIC
Sing the song "Go Tell' and march around, keeping rhythm with sticks.

Jesus Ascends into Heaven

Acts 1:1–11; Luke 24:44–53

Up a hill went Jesus with His disciples one day.
"Wait for the Holy Spirit," they heard the Lord say.

Walk in place; point up.

They were listening to Jesus and using their eyes.
Then Jesus, while speaking, went up to the sky!

Point to ears, then eyes; slowly raise both arms.

Suddenly, two angels were standing nearby.
They asked, "Why are you staring up at the sky?

Show 2 fingers; look surprised and point up.

This same Jesus will come back again someday."
Then the men went to the city to wait and to pray.

Nod head; walk in place.

This Jesus we love will come back for us too.
He'll take us to heaven as He promised to do.

Hug self and nod; point up.

LANGUAGE DEVELOPMENT
Talk about the up and down words used in the
rhyme. Think of other directional words.

THE HOLY SPIRIT LEADS THE APOSTLES

God Sends the Holy Spirit

Acts 2:1–21

After Jesus had risen and gone back to heaven, the disciples were gathered together in a special room waiting for the gift of the Holy Spirit. This is what happened when He came.

It sounded like a windstorm; a loud noise filled the air.
It looked like flames were resting on each head above their hair.

> *Sway back and forth; wiggle fingers above head.*

The Spirit filled each person so that they could speak God's Word.
They spoke to visitors from other lands, surprised by what they heard.

> *Put hands on chest; point to mouth.*

The visitors were so amazed, they asked, "How can this be?
We hear them speak the languages known just to you and me."

> *Hold arms, palms up, in surprise; point to others and to self.*

Then Peter gave a sermon that said God's Spirit would come.
That Spirit would help God's people tell just what Jesus had done.

> *Hook thumbs and wave fingers, moving hands downward for descending dove; point to mouth.*

The Holy Spirit is God's gift who brings
     faith to you too.
Through God's Word and His
     Sacraments, He calls and gathers you.

> *Show open Bible; hug self.*

CREATIVE EXPRESSION
Draw a picture of the story.

Peter and John Heal the Lame Man

Acts 3

To the temple went Peter and John to pray.
"Please give me some money," they heard a man say.

    Fold hands to beg; point to ear.

This beggar just sat—couldn't walk, leap, or run.
He only sat begging; it wasn't much fun.

    Point to feet; hold out hands.

"I can't give you money," said Peter that day.
"Get up and go walk, for God healed you. Hooray!"

    Shake head no; show "rise up" with hands, then walk in place.

The man left him walking and leaping away.
He was praising the Lord as he walked off that day.

    Walk and leap.

God has healed you too; He sent Jesus, His Son.
When He died on the cross, forgiveness He won.

    Point to others; make cross with fingers; clap.

COUNTING/GROSS-MOTOR SKILLS
Have children choose a number and then jump in place that many times. Pick a different number and step in place or leap or skip.

God's Servant Stephen

Acts 6–7

In the Book of Acts, we hear how quickly God's Word spread.
We hear of Stephen's service and what Stephen boldly said.

> *Open hands like book; point to ears, then mouth.*

Not everyone was happy to hear of sin and Jesus' grace.
Since they were very angry, God took Stephen from that place.

> *Cover ears, shake head no; point up.*

God is taking care of us when bad things happen too.
He knows when we are hurt or sad and don't know what to do.

> *Nod head yes and extend hands, palms up; draw tears on face.*

Tell God when you're worried and tell Him when you're sad.
He will always care for you and that can make you glad.

> *Point to mouth; hug self and smile.*

SPIRITUAL DEVELOPMENT

Write the children's worries and fears on word bubbles (or paper stones). Post them around a cross as you talk about God's care. Say 1 Peter 5:7 together.

Philip and the Ethiopian

Acts 8:26–40

A man from Ethiopia was going home one day.
He just had left Jerusalem, where he had gone to pray.
  Bounce, hold reins.

Isaiah's words were written down upon the scroll he read.
"I wish that there was someone here explaining this," he said.
  Elbows at side, palms up.

But he was in a wilderness, with chariots and men.
Where could he find someone to explain the scroll to him?
  Tap head, look puzzled.

Philip then came to him, sent by the Holy Spirit.
"I'll explain Isaiah's words, if you would like to hear it.
  Hand out offering to help.

The man Isaiah wrote about has risen from the grave.
His name is Jesus Christ, the Lord, and He has come to save."
  Make cross with fingers.

"Philip, will you baptize me? For I believe the Word.
I will share what you have said with those who have not heard."
  Pour water on head.

Children, let's go tell the world, empowered by the Spirit,
Of the love of Jesus Christ, so they may gladly hear it.
  Beckon with hand.

SOCIAL STUDIES
Before computers and books, people wrote on flattened plants or animal skins and rolled them up. Use light brown construction paper cut in half lengthwise and paper-towels rolls. Have children draw a picture of something they like. Roll up the paper on the rolls. Trade and unroll paper to "read" the pictures.

Dorcas

Acts 9:36–43

Dorcas was a woman who followed Jesus Christ.
She helped the poor and needy, did things both kind and nice.
> *Put hand on heart.*

But one day she grew ill, so ill that she would die.
Her friends came to her funeral, to mourn and say good-bye.
> *Draw tears on face with fingers.*

Peter, Christ's disciple, was also there that day.
He sent those mourning outside, and he began to pray.
> *Fold hands in prayer.*

He called her by her other name, said, "Tabitha, arise."
By God's great power, at his words, she opened up her eyes.
> *Close eyes; then open them.*

She sat up right away, and Peter took her hand.
He showed her to believers. Their joy spread through the land!
> *Jump and clap.*

For Christ had given power to those who followed Him.
He told them they would heal the sick and raise the dead again.
> *Point to heaven.*

Each time that His disciples would heal or raise someone,
The people knew that Jesus was truly God's own Son.
> *Nod yes.*

Each time we hear these stories, we see what God has done.
We, too, believe in Jesus. He's truly God's own Son.
> *Point to ears; cross hands over heart and nod yes.*

SOCIAL STUDIES

Helping the sick is a way to show God's love.
Set up a doll and stuffed-animal hospital with
bandages, tape, blankets, and a play medical kit.

Peter and Cornelius

Acts 10

Cornelius was a Roman, a brave centurion.
He worshiped God and prayed to Him, gave help to everyone.
> *Make muscles; fold hands in prayer.*

An angel of the Lord said to him one day,
"The Lord says talk to Peter. Go find him right away."
> *Point to mouth; point out.*

Cornelius told his men. "It's Peter I must see.
Please search until you find him. Ask him to come to me."
> *Point to mouth; shade eyes with hand, searching.*

Meanwhile, a dream showed Peter God sent His only Son
To save all people who believe, no matter where they're from.
> *Make cross with fingers.*

For Peter once believed the Lord was not for others.
But Jesus showed him how to love the Romans as his brothers.
> *Point up and then around room, shaking head no; point up and cross hands on heart.*

So Peter met Cornelius, and when he preached God's Word,
Cornelius and other people were saved through what they heard.
> *Hold hands like open book; open arms to welcome all.*

MISSIONS
Put a sticky note on a foreign country on a globe. Then put the globe in a corner. Next, explain what missionaries do. Play follow the leader around the room until you arrive at the globe. Sing "Jesus Loves the Little Children." Talk about children living in different countries around the world.

Peter's Escape from Prison

Acts 12

When Herod was the king, the Christian faith was tested.
He hunted Christians down and then had them arrested.
Pound fists on palm.

Peter, too, was captured. To him the guards would say,
"We'll chain and watch you closely. You'll never get away!"
Point finger; shake head no.

Though Herod put him in a jail, God set Peter free.
An angel made the chains fall off and said, "Now, follow me."
Pretend to push chains off hands.

They walked unseen, right past the guards; the gate unlocked itself.
Soon Peter, rescued, in the street, was standing by himself.
Tiptoe in place.

He went to Mary's house, a place he'd been before.
The maid was so surprised, she wouldn't open up the door!
Knock; put hands on side of face, surprised.

"I just heard Peter's voice!" the others she would tell.
"That can't be right," they told her. "He's locked up in a cell!"
Shake head no.

Peter kept on knocking until they let him in.
He told how God had set him free, for God will always win.
Knock and open door; point to heaven.

Peter kept on preaching. The Christians would not hide,
For every chain is broken when God is on your side.
Pat selves on back and nod.

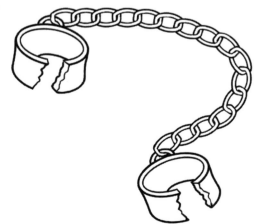

DRAMATIC PLAY
Using strips of construction paper and glue sticks, teach students to make a
six-link paper chain. Reread the poem and break chains on the last section.
Place broken chains around the room or on the room altar.

~~~~~~
PAUL'S MISSION AND LETTERS
~~~~~~

The Conversion of Paul

Acts 9:1–31

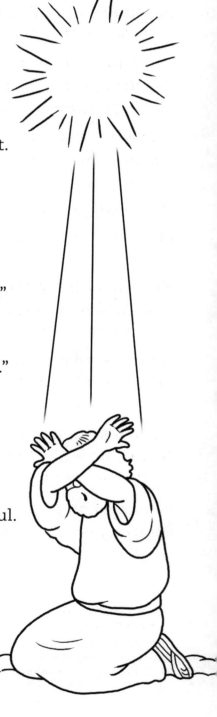

You've heard of Saul, the king. Now meet a different Saul.
This Saul was mean to Christians and tried to hurt them all.
> *Make a mean face.*

Saul thought what he was doing was truly good and right.
He thought that hurting Christians was pleasing in God's sight.
> *Nod head and point up.*

One day while walking to a town, he saw a flash so bright.
He fell upon the ground in fear, was blinded by the light.
> *Fall to ground.*

A voice said, "I am Jesus, the one you're trying to hurt.
Go wait in town for my next words; now rise up from the dirt."
> *Get up.*

The Lord sent Ananias to baptize Saul and to heal,
"Saul, you'll get your sight back. Now serve the Lord with zeal."
> *Make sign of the cross for "baptize"; close eyes, then open them.*

The Holy Spirit entered, restored the sight to Saul.
Saul was sent both far and wide to share God's Word with all.
> *Walk in place.*

God's love can change the meanies, even those like Saul.
You may have heard his other name; we know him best as Paul.
> *Cross hands over heart and nod.*

SOCIAL DEVELOPMENT
Playact solve-it situations. Have children stand on a "solve-it"
rug when they have a disagreement and try to first solve it by
themselves without an adult's help.

Paul and Barnabas

Acts 13–14

Paul and Barnabas traveled here and there,
    Telling people everywhere,
      Point right, then left; cup hands around mouth.

"Jesus died to take our sins away,
So we can live in heaven one day."
      Make sign of the cross; point up.

DRAMATIC PLAY
Role-play telling others about Jesus.

Paul and Timothy

Acts 15:1–16:5

Imagine way back when, there were no telephones,
No Internet, no TV, just word of mouth alone.
      Touch mouth.

There were no cars, or radios, or movies at the mall.
God's helpers walked from town to town to spread the Word to all.
      Walk in place.

A mother and grandmother heard Paul would come that day.
They opened up their home to him and welcomed him to stay.
      Open door.

CREATIVE EXPRESSION
Use construction-paper strips to make a paper chain to show how people tell others about Jesus. Have children write their name on a strip and add it to the chain. Add other family names or names of friends.

And so, young Timothy met Paul and said, "Let's begin.
I want to help you in your work, so all are saved from sin."
      Shake hand.

The two men worked for God, becoming friends quite dear.
Young Timothy and Paul preached of Jesus far and near.
      Cross hands over heart; walk in place.

We thank You, Jesus, for the ones that helped Your kingdom grow.
Use us, as well, to build Your Church, so everyone may know.
      Fold hands in prayer; point to others.

Lydia Is Baptized

Acts 16:11–15

A woman, Lydia by name, sold purple goods for trade.
She loved the Lord and served Him with the money that she made.

Cross hands over chest; open hands to serve.

When Paul told Lydia of Jesus, God spoke to her heart.
Her whole family was baptized, and then she played a part.

Make cross with fingers and point to heart; make sign of the cross.

She offered Paul a place to stay. And with the help she gave,
It made it easier for Paul to tell folks Jesus saves.

Hold arms out, palms up; point to mouth and make cross with fingers.

We, too, can share God's Word and cheer each other on,
Till everyone meets Jesus and trusts in God the Son.

Hold hands like open book and nod; point to others and cross hands over chest.

SOCIAL DEVELOPMENT
Let children tell what they would like to be when they grow up. Talk about how to serve God in those professions. During free time, provide dress-up items for various professions.

Paul and Silas in Prison

Acts 16:16–40

A girl who was a slave made money telling men
What she saw the future had in store for them.
> *Count money in hand.*

When she met Paul and Silas, she began to shout,
"These men tell how God saves," and daily, she'd cry out.
> *Cup hands around mouth.*

Paul saw she had a spirit: "By Jesus, leave her be!"
The spirit left, but now the girl, the future could not see.
> *Shake finger sternly; shake head no.*

Her owners got quite angry. "You made our business fail!
We'll show you troublemakers! We'll send you straight to jail!"
> *Look angry, hands on hips.*

They locked them in a prison and bound their feet with chains.
Still Paul and Silas trusted God to help them through this pain.
> *Put chains on feet; cross hands over heart.*

Suddenly, an earthquake set the prisoners free.
Paul and Silas did not run; the jailer was relieved.
> *Shake and fall to ground.*

The jailer then was baptized, and later the next day,
Paul and Silas were released to go upon their way.
> *Make sign of the cross; walk in place.*

Should you be in trouble, remember and believe,
"I can do all things, through Christ, the one who strengthens me."
> *Point to head on "believe"; point to self, make cross with fingers, muscle arms.*

LANGUAGE DEVELOPMENT
Go through the alphabet and find words that rhyme with the word *bad*. Pray to God to help you if you are scared. Also tell an adult about it.

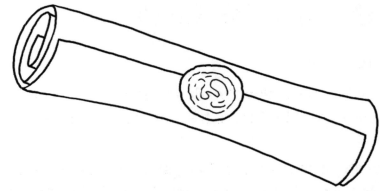

Philemon

The Book of Philemon

Paul wrote a letter to a friend, and in it he would plead
For a favor from this friend to help someone in need.
Write.

"Philemon, I have with me, your slave Onesimus.
I know he ran away from you, and he has lost your trust.
Run in place.

He has become a Christian; He loves the Lord, it's true.
And though I'd love to keep him here, I'm sending him to you.
Open hands.

He comes back like a brother, and helpful he will be.
Please welcome him with open arms, as you would welcome me.
Open arms in welcome.

If he should owe you money or has hurt you any way,
I will pay all that he owes, when next I come to stay.
Count money in hand.

By sending him to you, I'm sending you my heart.
In Christ, he's been made useful, and now he'll do his part."
Put hands on heart.

For all of us are useless, until made whole by Him.
Jesus gave His life for ours and freed us from our sin.
Make cross with fingers.

ENVIRONMENT/SPIRITUAL DEVELOPMENT
Catch sow bugs, roly-polys, or grasshoppers and put them in a jar. We are stewards of creation. Talk about how it is okay to look at bugs but then we should let them go. Do not let bugs die in a jar.

Paul Sails for Rome

Acts 27

Paul was a prisoner; at times his life was hard.
He set sail for a trial, under Roman guard.

> *Say, "Splish splash."*

Paul said, "Dock the ship for now. We should not sail this late.
The waters will get rougher, and the winter will not wait."

> *Use hands to make rough waves.*

But no one listened to him, so fierce winds blew and tossed.
The ship could not be steered. They thought that all was lost.

> *Make wind noises.*

The sun and stars were blotted out; it seemed the end was near.
But God sent Paul an angel, who said they should not fear.

> *Use hands to make angel wings.*

Paul said, "We will lose the ship, but God is on our side.
So eat some food, keep up your strength. God says we will not die."

> *Point up; make muscle arms.*

The ship was smashed upon the reef, and just as God had said,
Everyone survived the wreck, not one of them was dead.

> *Swim.*

When trouble comes your way, and you are feeling blue,
Just remember God is there. Trust Him to see you through.

> *Point up, then cross hands over heart.*

SAFETY
Go over water-safety rules. Practice putting on child life vest.

The Bible Tells Us So

The Book of Acts

In Paul's work and on Paul's way,
God was with him every day.
In Paul's sorrows, joys, and fears,
He was glad that God was near.
Yes, Jesus loves him.
    Yes, Jesus loves him.
Yes, Jesus loves him, the Bible tells us so.

In my work and on my way,
God is with me every day.
In my sorrows, joys, and fears,
I am glad that God is near.
Yes, Jesus loves me.
    Yes, Jesus loves me.
Yes, Jesus loves me, the Bible tells us so.

MUSIC
Sing the poem to the tune of "Jesus Loves Me, This I Know."

HEAVEN IS OUR HOME

John's Vision of Heaven

Revelation 21–22

An angel came to John, to show him heav'nly things.
John wrote down what he saw and how the Lord would reign.
Make angel wings with hands; write.

He saw the brand-new heaven and earth without the tears.
There was no sin or evil, and nothing there to fear.
Point to eyes and draw tears on face; shake head no.

He saw a holy city that gleamed and sparkled bright.
The streets of gold and pearly gates gave off a dazzling light!
Point to eyes; make twinkle fingers.

He saw all kinds of jewels, twinkling in the walls.
The sunlight was not needed; God's glory lit it all.
Point to eyes; shield eyes from bright light.

He saw a throne with Jesus, his Savior and his Friend,
Surrounded by the saints, singing praises without end.
Point to eyes and cross hands over heart; sing.

So, Jesus, when the time comes to take my heavenly place,
I, too, will thank and praise You when I see You face-to-face!
Point up; fold hands in prayer.

MUSIC/ART
Sing the hymn "Have No Fear, Little Flock." Have children draw a picture of heaven.